Finding Your Way
in the Outdoors

An Outdoor Life Book

Finding Your Way in the Outdoors

Compass Navigation
Map Reading • Route Finding
Weather Forecasting

by Robert L. Mooers, Jr.

Drawings by
George J. Killion, Jr.

OUTDOOR LIFE BOOKS

To Bill Bendy . . . as good a man who ever lived; and to Evelyn, Lucile, and Mike, the climbing friends who inspired this book; and last but not least, to "Perky," who held my lap in place while the job got done.

Contents

Acknowledgments

To Mr. Robert Kitchen for his criticism of technical content; to Miss Connie Fulgum for her work on composition; to Charles Teague and William Mohr for their generous photographical talents; to Mr. R.C. Dinsmore of the Dinsmore Instrument Company for his helpful correspondence; to Leupold and Stevens Instruments, Inc. for their technical support; and to Recreational Equipment, Inc., Seattle, for indulging me in a lengthy examination of their entire stock of compasses — to all who helped in any way — my thanks and appreciation.

Finding Your Way
in the Outdoors

Introduction

There are few experiences which quite compare with successfully leading the way over a wilderness route. A happy ending to an outdoor adventure brings a feeling of satisfaction and self-sufficiency to the navigator. With the help of the magnetic compass, success is made more probable (though never assured) and utter failure is rarely a serious matter.

But does the weekend or once-a-year adventurer really need the help of a compass? Most of us will never set foot in the wilderness of untracked barrens or deep jungles. The answer is that a wilderness is *any* place where the consequences of becoming lost may be serious or even unpleasant. Such a place might be a few square miles of a public park or the back forty acres of a farm. The most innocuous route may contain pitfalls. Intervening hills, trees, and winding detours may hide the objective long enough to confuse you. Most dangerous of all, especially at higher elevations, is the ever-present possibility of bad weather.

This book has been written for the beginning navigator who wants to understand his own particular type of compass. It also has in mind the otherwise capable outdoorsman who, although already familiar with compass work, is confused on one or a number of points.

Number one among these sources of confusion is the fact that while all compasses are designed to do the same things, there are at least three fundamentally different types in current use. Instruction often comes from friends, treachers, and authors who discuss "the compass" as though all were nearly identical. Even the best books on wilderness navigation do not go sufficiently into the actual reading and working of the various types. The fact is that any of these three significantly different types taken alone can be confusing enough. With directions lumped together, the compass can overwhelm the beginner and cause him to drop out of the activity, or worse, prompt him to go ahead inadequately prepared.

Another source of confusion stems from instructions printed by manufacturers of compasses. Understandably, because each company cannot write book-length directions (and because it wants the minimum number of "easy" steps), instructions stress the mechanics of operation without developing the reasons for each step. Many mistakes issue from not fully knowing why a step is taken, especially under the trying conditions which so often occur in the outdoors.

Finally, a note on practice. Practice . . . and learn. No amount of detailed explanation is any good without it.

How to Use This Book

This book has two purposes: (1) to explain how to *read* a compass; (2) to explain how to *use* it in finding your way in the wilds in conjunction with maps and nature's signs.

There are three basic types of compasses. Each type is widely used in recreation, as well as in professional fields. To use this book effectively, check your compass against the following descriptions, then skip the two chapters which do not deal with your own model. Have your compass handy during all of your reading.

Type A Compass—Chapter 2

Any compass having (1) a *clockwise* degree system, from 0° around to the right; (2) a magnetic needle which operates *independently* of the compass card. (Skip Chapters 3 and 4.)

Type B Compass—Chapter 3

Any compass in which the compass card *and* the magnetic needle are joined and work as a unit. (Skip Chapters 2 and 4.)

Type C Compass — Chapter 4

Any compass having a reversed, or counterclock-wise, degree numbering system, from 0° around to the left. (Skip Chapters 2 and 3.)

Except for the skipped chapters, the rest of the book applies to all compasses. The reader is encouraged to begin by reading through the Glossary to become familiar with terms as they will be used.

Glossary

AGONIC LINE (*a-gone-ick*). An imaginary line along which Magnetic North coincides with True North. A line of no declination.

AZIMUTH (*az-muhth*). A straight-line compass direction between two points. Usually called a bearing.

BACK BEARING. The reverse degree value of a bearing, 180° in the opposite direction.

BACKSIGHT. The taking of a reading on an identifiable landmark at or toward the rear of the starting position. It is used in holding to the line of travel both leaving and returning to the starting position.

BEARING. Generally understood to mean any compass direction from 0° to 360°. Technically, however, a bearing is a specially written degree reading based upon the quadrant system. For example, S 20° E (read 'south 20° east') is a direction lying 20° to the east of south. It does no harm to refer to a compass direction, actually written in azimuth form, as a bearing as long as the reader recognizes a reading in either form. The Appendix contains a section on the bearing (or quadrant) numbering system.

BRACKETING. Planning a course in relation to (rather than directly toward) either a natural feature or a marker placed by the navigator to facilitate the return trip. Used in featureless terrain or woods.

CALIBRATION. The scale or numbering system on the compass card.

CARD. The compass card. The numbered plate either fixed to the compass housing or allowed to rotate on the center pivot with the magnetized needle. Imprinted on it is the degree system from which readings are taken.

CARDINAL POINTS. The four principal compass points of north, south, east, and west.

CENTER PIVOT. The post upon which the compass needle rests. The center post allows the needle to maintain its magnetic orientation while the housing is rotated.

COMPASS CARD. See CARD.

COMPASS DIAL. A compass card which can be rotated to offset magnetic declination. Found on specialized compasses.

DAMPER. A device built into a compass and used to slow the oscillations of the needle. There are two kinds of dampers in wide use, liquid and mechanical, and both use the friction principle. A third type, gaining favor for its speed, is called induction damping. This works on the principle of induced magnetism, i.e., the magnetism induced in a metal when it comes into the magnetic field of a magnet.

DECLINATION. The amount by which the compass needle tilts away from True North due to the direction of the earth's magnetic lines of force at a given place. Declination is specified as east or west. *See* AGONIC LINE.

DEGREE. One of the 360 equal angular divisions of a circle. "Degree" is indicated by a small "o" to the right of a number, e.g., 35°.

DEVIATION. The amount of declination due to *local* magnetic influences (such as lodestone or iron ore deposits, electrical devices and power lines, or metals too close to the compass.) Deviation may increase or decrease the known declination by significant amounts. Known deviation areas are sometimes marked on maps, but more often the possibility of its influence must be kept in mind. In Chapter 5 a method for checking on the total amount of difference between True and Magnetic North will be given.

FIELD BEARING. A compass reading taken in progress as opposed to one taken from the map.

FORESTER'S COMPASS. A compass having a reversed numbering system, read from 0° to the left.

HOUSING. The outer container of the working compass. The housing often plays a role in sighting the compass.

INTER-CARDINAL POINTS. The four compass directions halfway between the cardinal points. They are northeast, southeast, southwest, and northwest.

INTERSECTION. The technique of plotting a remote point position by means of crossed bearings sighted from two or more locations.

ISOGONIC LINE (*ice-oh-gone'-ick*). A line along which the angle between True North and Magnetic North is the same.

LENSATIC COMPASS, or lens-sight type. A TYPE B COMPASS with a special sighting combination for increasing the accuracy of readings. Most are of military design.

LUBBER'S LINE. A line painted on the deck of a ship (in early days of sailing). It passed from the bow through the center of the wheel house and was used as a reference point for determining the angle between magnetic direction and the ship's direction. The old salts ridiculed its use, hence the term "lubber's" line. Many modern compasses have sighting lines which serve the same useful function.

MAGNETIC FIELD. The magnetic field of the earth, with one pole in the Northern Hemisphere and one in the Southern Hemisphere. The whole system functions like a complicated version of an ordinary bar magnet.

MAGNETIC MERIDIAN. A line which crosses the True meridian at an angle equal to the magnetic declination in the area covered by the map.

MAGNETIC NORTH. The area of northern convergence of the lines of force in the earth's magnetic field. It is an area rather than a point location and is to be found some 1,300 miles from the True or geographic North Pole.

MAP BEARING. A compass reading taken from a map. It differs from a field bearing in that it need not consider magnetic declination. All that is needed is the angle between the objective and True North, measured from the map position of the navigator.

MERIDIAN. Any of the theoretical lines running from the True North Pole to the True South Pole of the earth as shown on maps.

NEEDLE. The magnetic compass needle, which is balanced on a pivot allowing it to maintain a northerly orientation. The north-indicating end of the needle is usually darkened, striped, arrow-shaped, or lettered "N" to prevent confusion with the south-indicating end.

NORTH-SOUTH LINE. The True North-South line on a compass card (which differs according to the type of compass design) or any meridian on a map.

OBJECTIVE. The final destination or, if that is out of view, an intermediary point toward which one is navigating.

OBSERVER'S MERIDIAN. The observer's line of sight toward True North; i.e., the line which passes through the True North Pole, the observer, and the True South Pole.

ORIENTATION. Refers to the location or placement of one object in the navigational picture in relation to another. Usually it means the location of True North with respect to the navigator, compass in hand, or the location of True North with respect to a map.

POINT-LINE. The straight line in which the navigator, the compass, and the objective must be aligned for a reading to be properly taken or used. The concept will be slightly altered for the use of the Forester's compass.

PRE-TRIP PLAN. A map study and sketch of the proposed route of travel including compass readings taken from map detail.

RESECTION. The technique of plotting point position by means of crossed *back bearings* taken from the place where they intersect.

ROUTE. A point-to-point plan of travel not involving the extensive use of prepared trails. Routes begin where trails end.

ROUTE-FINDING. The broader task of guiding which includes navigation. Route-finding implies decisions on the technical feasibility of taking one direction over another. Navigation implies holding to the direction decided upon.

TAKING A BEARING. Sighting and reading the compass to find the degree value of a chosen reference feature.

TICK MARK. Short lines of varied lengths which represent numbers of degrees on the compass card. Usually, the shortest tick mark' represents one, two, or five degrees, depending upon the particular design.

TRUE NORTH. The geographic top of the earth. It is the point of axis in the Northern Hemisphere about which the earth rotates (in an easterly direction).

TYPE A COMPASS. In this book, any compass having a clockwise numbering system in which the needle works independently of the compass card. The compass card will be fixed to the housing. This includes most field compasses, in popular use.

TYPE B COMPASS. In this book, any compass on which the compass card *and* the compass needle are joined and work together — that is, card and needle maintain the magnetic orientation. This includes the lensatic compass and most auto, marine, and aeronautical compasses.

TYPE C COMPASS. In this book, any compass having a reversed or counterclockwise numbering system. This includes the Forester's and Cruiser's compasses.

USING A BEARING. Determining an unknown direction by sighting along the line of a known degree value.

VARIATION. A synonym for declination, taken from the fact that for a given area Magnetic North (or Mag North) "varies" from True North by so many degrees. Both terms are correct, but for consistency, this book will use "declination" throughout.

1 / How a Compass Works

As with many of man's fundamental inventions, the origins of the magnetic compass are lost in the haze of history's early dawn. We have accounts of early impressions of the nature of magnetism, and we have a few early dates for its use in navigation, but these are not as exciting as would be the full story of how the principle finally filled the need.

Natural magnetism is a property of lodestone, or magnetite as it is known today. Uses for this mysterious power were found in religion, faith healing, and sorcery long before they were found in science. It is really no wonder. Such bedeviled forces were obviously nothing for the layman to dabble with. Those who dared undoubtedly risked censure and even bodily punishment by religious and civil officials.

In the days of Egypt's pharaohs, for example, a scientific proposal for using rocks to tell direction would have ranked with Galileo's report of mountains on the moon and Fulton's funny steamboat as national jokes.

It was not until the known world became much larger than the Mediterranean area that the scientific use of magnetism really found its place in the compass. The directional property of lodestone had long been known and crude compasses were even in use, but the need was simply not critical. Winds in the Mediterranean Sea generally blow one way. Sailors had only to follow the wind to go south, and tack back against it to go north. East-west routes pretty much followed the coastline. But by the beginning of the fourteenth century, the need for a reliable navigational instrument had become acute. The historical forces which produced this need are too complex to trace here. However, we can pinpoint certain developments: The voyages of Marco Polo, which set the West on fire to bring back the riches of the Orient; Europe's new concept of the large standing army, which tied military spending to the race across the seas for colonies and gold; and the spirit of the Renaissance, with its emphasis on man and worldly knowledge.

Such forces do not go unanswered, and by 1297, just two years after Polo's return from the court of Kublai Khan, the pivot compass had been invented. A century later it was standard equipment on all English ships, ships which ruled the seas from the destruction of the Spanish Armada in 1588 to the present century. Even this great step in compass development was a refinement of knowledge which had existed for ages.

Figure 1. The simplest form of magnetic compass, not as convenient but every bit as reliable as the most sophisticated modern compass. The needle has been magnetized by stroking it, in one direction only, with a bar magnet.

No one knows when, but at some point in prehistory man made two important discoveries about lodestone: (1) that properly suspended this material really did indicate a north-south direction; (2) that a piece of iron, when rubbed against a chunk of lodestone, would take on the properties of magnetism.

The earliest navigational aids took two forms. Arab mariners of the eleventh century A.D. were known to have used the string suspension method. The Chinese version took the form of a *south*-pointing arrow floated on a straw in a bowl of water (*Figure 1*). This design was used up until the seventeenth century in China.

The magnetic compass has changed little in hundreds of years. Rather, the greatest changes have been in our knowledge of the behavior of the magnetism by which it works, and this is a tribute to the marvelous simplicity of the instrument itself.

The Modern Compass

Physically, a modern magnetic compass consists of a housing and two important components. One of these is the magnetized needle. The other is the circular compass card with the degree values which make the needle's direction meaningful. *Figure 2* is an exploded view of a typical simple compass.

The compass card contains a circle which is divided into 360°. Each two degrees, or five or even ten on some models, is shown by a short line called a *tick*. At intervals of 15° or 20° a longer tick with a printed number is shown to help in reading degree values. Most models have capital letters at 90° intervals to denote the cardinal directions.

The degree values of the cardinal points should be learned thoroughly. They are north (N) at 0°; east

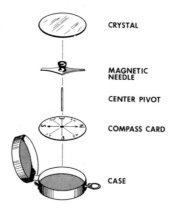

Figure 2. An exploded view of a basic modern magnetic compass. Construction details differ, but all models use these simple components.

(E) at 90°; south (S) at 180°; and west (W) at 270°. These, along with the intercardinal points halfway between, are the main reference points. Having them firmly in mind will save time and confusion. For example, a reading of 85° should immediately direct one's attention to a bit north of east.

The circle on the compass card is a sort of model of the circular nature of anyone's full 360° field of view. The whole idea of using the compass lies in fitting this model to the real earth—in exactly the same way each time the compass is used. Once this fit is made, the navigator may sight on any object and read its degree value on the compass card along the line of sight (*Figure 3*). The compass card allows the assigning of number names to objects and directions, making it much easier to communicate them to others or to record them for the future.

The most important property of the degree system is that each bearing taken from a given position is completely unique. From the bird feeder on the back lawn, the big sycamore in the pasture is exactly 128°. From the garden's southern corner, however, the bearing becomes 125°. Readings on specific objects will change only when the navigator changes his sighting position. The navigator in *Figure 4* may well have found his "starting position" by being directed to "find the place where the fire lookout is due north and High Peak is 30°." No other position on earth will satisfy those directions. Later we will study this method of plotting and finding positions.

Without a definite way of fitting the compass card to true directions the instrument would be of little value. This is the function of the compass needle. It points out Magnetic North, and once he knows how far Magnetic North is from True North, the navigator

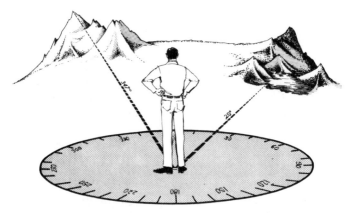

Figure 3. When a compass is in reading position it is as though the navigator stands in the center-pivot position. From there, anything in his view may be lined up with a degree value, and anything not in his view may be reached if its degree value is known.

can easily orient his compass card to all other true directions.

Magnetism

The role of magnetism in the hand compass is so vital to a proper understanding of compass use that we should take a closer look at it before going into the actual reading of the various types. When two magnets are placed close together (such as when suspended from strings) their opposite poles (or ends) will be drawn together while their like poles will repel each other. A single bar magnet can be shown to have a definite pattern of magnetic power. Iron filings sprinkled around a bar magnet will arrange themselves in lines called *magnetic lines of force,* thought to flow from the magnet's south pole to its

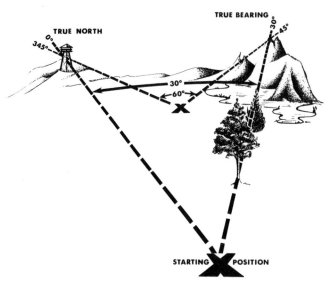

Figure 4. Bearings taken from a given sighting position are exclusive. They can only be changed by moving to a different place on the earth's surface.

north pole. When a second magnet enters the magnetic field of one more powerful than itself, its south pole will attempt to swing around and align itself with the north-seeking lines of force.

The earth itself acts much like a huge bar magnet having north and south magnetic poles and a definite but complex magnetic field. The earth's magnetic energy influences and is influenced by all other magnetic materials on and above its surface. This of course includes the tiny bar magnet that serves as a compass needle. Allowed to freely pivot within its housing, the needle continuously aligns itself with the earth's magnetic lines of force in a general north-south direction.

It is obviously important to know which end of the needle is which. The north-indicating end is usually marked in some manner. It may be red, or just darker; it may be striped; or it may even be marked with an "N." Some are shaped like an arrow. This simple test can be made if there are any doubts. Face the morning sun with the compass held in front of you; the end of the needle pointing to your left will be the north-seeking end. In the afternoon this will of course be reversed.

The Two Norths

For many reasons only partly understood, the earth's magnetic field is not a very stable one. Chapter 5 is a longer discussion of this fascinating subject, but for now let us accept the statement that Magnetic North is not alone reliable enough to be the sole basis for compass navigation. What is needed is a fixed point, one which never changes. This point is True North, the geographic north pole of the earth. The compass will locate Magnetic North, and using this information, the navigator can locate True North and line it up with 0° on his compass card.

Keeping track of Magnetic North, which differs from place to place and even from time to time, is a matter of constant measurement and record keeping. The U.S. government publishes this information periodically and it is very easy to obtain. In addition, all U.S. Geological Survey maps contain the necessary information for their area of coverage.

Magnetic North is located about 1,300 miles from the True North Pole, and is currently in northern Canada. It is an area rather than a point location, for it is the area of convergence of the earth's magnetic

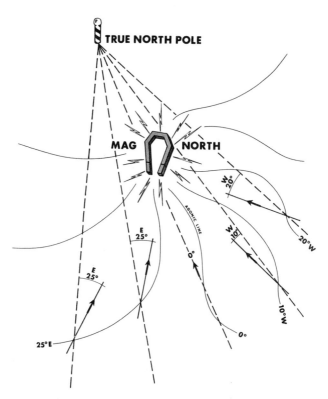

Figure 5. Magnetic declination is the same at all points along isogonic lines (arrows). Note that the lines themselves do *not* give direction.

lines of force. The difference between True North and the direction indicated by the compass needle is called magnetic *declination;* that is, the needle declines away from True North by a certain number of degrees. Declination will be either east or west depending on what part of the world one is in. In the United States, for those living on the west side of the *agonic line* (the line of zero declination) declination

19

MAGNETIC DECLINATION IN THE UNITED STATES

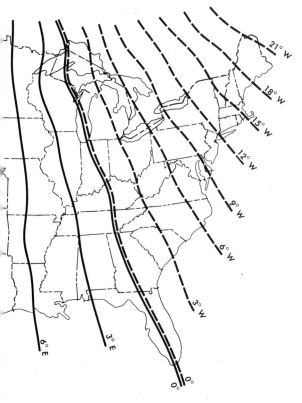

Figure 6. A map of magnetic declinations in the
United States, current as of 1970. Surveys are
taken and published every five years by the
Coast and Geodedic Survey. Values east of the
agonic line (doubled) are *west* declinations and
those west of the line are *east* declinations. Be
aware of significant local deviations.

will be *east.* Magnetic North will be to the east of True North. The reverse is true for those living to the east of the agonic line. The principle of declination is shown in *Figure 5*.

Figure 6 is a map of the United States showing approximate declination across the country. There are many exceptions, so actual magnetic declination should be taken from a much more detailed U.S.G.S. topographic map. The lines on the maps *are not* magnetic lines of force. They are isogonic lines, which means that readings taken at all points represented by one particular line will be the same. They will show the same angle between True North and Magnetic North. Except for a narrow strip along an *agonic* line, magnetic declination must always be allowed for in using the compass.

Warning: The compass needle will *tend* toward Magnetic North, but it will actually register the direction of strongest magnetic influence wherever it may be. Any extraneous magnetic source can dominate or seriously affect the direction indicated by the needle. Slightly magnetized metals on or near the navigator, natural deposits of lodestone or iron ore, and electrical devices and facilities (such as power lines) are frequent mischief makers. The photoelectric cell in light meters is especially troublesome; so are nails or screws in desk tops, tables, and flooring.

Taken together these extra magnetic sources are called magnetic *deviation.* Most can be avoided with simple caution, and in a later chapter we will present a method for measuring the unavoidable sources of deviation. Once it is known it can be added to the amount of declination and treated, as we shall see, in the same way.

2 / *The*
Type A
Compass

Check your compass once more to see that it fits this description. A TYPE A compass has:

1. A *clockwise* degree system (from 0° around to the right.)
2. A magnetic needle which operates *independently* of the compass card.

Representative TYPE A instruments appear in *Figure 7*. This is the most popular category of magnetic field compass in use today. It offers the navigator the distinct advantage of being able to read bearings in True form. Converting from Magnetic to True, one of the most troublesome aspects of reading the compass, is eliminated. The mechanical trait which gives TYPE A this ability is implied in the above description; that is, while its needle is free to main-

Figure 7. Three versions of the Type A compass. Note Direction-of-Travel arrow on the plastic base of model on left. This model is "damped" automatically by its liquid-filled housing. The other two are damped mechanically by a button on the side.

tain a Magnetic North orientation, its compass card can be oriented to True position. Bearings may then be read from the True-oriented card.

Many models of slightly differing design will fit the Type A definition. All will fit the directions in this chapter, but one particular design feature, the Direction-of-Travel Arrow, deserves a note of explanation. The instruments in *Figure 7* represent different design approaches to the Direction-of-Travel Arrow feature.*

A Direction-of-Travel Arrow is a built-in manually operated pointer which is used very much like a bookmark. The arrow itself trains the line of sight while

---

* See the Appendix, Compass Features to Look For When Buying, for comments on the DOT arrow and other specialized compass features.

its shaft or head, depending on the model, marks the desired bearing on the compass card. Throughout the chapter alternate steps marked "DOT arrow" will be included where appropriate, but it should be emphasized that this feature does not in itself change the workings of the TYPE A compass at all.

Orienting the Compass

Orienting the compass is implicit in taking and using compass bearings, but is somewhat of a separate process when orienting a map for field use or establishing general directions—getting one's bearings, so to speak. To orient the compass means to rotate its compass card until its cardinal directional symbols correspond to the earth's True geographic directions. The magnetic compass needle will be used to locate the reference point, True North, by which this is done.

In order to orient the compass to True North, the navigator must know the magnetic declination in his area of operation. Study again *Figure 6,* the map of the United States showing current magnetic declination every few degrees of change across the country. In Seattle, Washington, for example, the magnetic needle will decline 22° *east* of True North. East declination will be the general rule for any area on the left side of the *agonic line* (the line of zero declination), which is shown in *Figure 6* running from Lake Michigan to southeast Florida.* On the right side of the agonic line the needle will decline some degrees *west* of True North.

---

* There are numerous exceptions to this "rule." Wise use of the map and other directional clues is always called for.

To Orient the Compass:

1. Determine the proper amount and direction of declination.
2. Hold the compass flat in the palm of the hand and look directly down on the compass card.
3. Rotate the compass card until 0° and the needle are separated by the amount and direction of magnetic declination (the DOT arrow need not be considered).

Examples:

For 22° *east* declination the needle is on 22°.
For 15° *west* declination the needle is on 345°.

The navigator must constantly be on his guard for sources of extra-magnetic influence. Review Chapter 1 and see Chapter 5 for discussions of magnetic declination and its more troublesome partner, magnetic *deviation*.

Reading a Type A Compass

Reading a compass is the process of associating one of its degree values with a particular ground direction. This occurs in two field situations: taking a bearing on a known objective, and using a bearing to locate an unknown objective. Both of these are concerned with forming a line of the same three points, the only difference being which of the three is unknown. The three points, which we shall refer to as the point-line, are:

1. The navigator's starting position. (This is not map position, but simply where he stands. It is always "known.")
2. The reading on the compass card.
3. The objective.

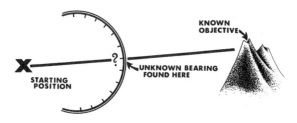

Figure 8. The point-line for *taking* a bearing with a TYPE A compass.

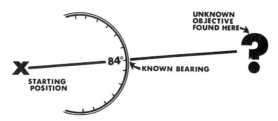

Figure 9. The point-line for *applying* a bearing with a TYPE A compass. Whether taking a bearing or using a predetermined one, the point-line is made up of the same three points. Two known quantities help to locate an unknown one.

Point-lines for the separate field situations of taking and using bearings are shown in *Figures 8* and *9*.

Here are the steps for each situation:

Field Situation #1: Taking a Bearing

The navigator *takes* a bearing when he can see a known objective and wishes to know its degree value.

1. Face the objective.
2. Orient the compass.

3. Sight over the center pivot (or rotate DOT arrow into sighting position).
4. Read the True bearing on the far side of the compass card along the line of sight (or at the DOT arrow).
5. Write it down. *Do not* trust it to memory. (Tired feet and carefree souls are poor memory aids.)

Field Situation #2: Using a Known Bearing

A known bearing may be obtained from a map, from a guidebook, or from the navigator's own previous route notes.

1. Orient the compass. (With DOT arrow: first turn the arrow to indicate the given bearing on the compass card.)
2. Sight over the given bearing (or along DOT arrow) in the new direction of travel.
3. Be certain compass is still properly oriented, then choose a landmark along the point-line. Make that the objective of this route segment.

There is of course a third field situation which occurs when the navigator has no bearing to follow and cannot see his objective either. This is more a matter of compass technique than of reading the instrument and it will be covered in Chapter 9. Another compass use, taking a bearing from a map, uses the compass card as a protractor and does not employ the magnetic principles of the compass itself. The process is the same for any instrument so is explained in Chapter 6, Maps and Map Reading, in the section on map direction.

Orienting a Map for Field Use

Before a map can be of use in the field it must be keyed to the earth's True geographic directions. Map detail will then coincide with ground detail and the map can be used to identify significant route features.

U.S.G.S. topographic maps have declination diagrams which make map orientation easy. The diagram consists of two lines joined at an angle equaling the magnetic declination for the particular sheet concerned. Use the declination diagram for orienting a map by following these steps:

1. Place compass center pivot on point of declination diagram angle.
2. Rotate compass until its north-south line (0°-180°) coincides with the diagram's True North line.
3. Rotate map (simultaneously with compass) until compass needle coincides with the diagram's Magnetic North line.

When using maps not having a declination diagram, work from a map meridian in the same manner. Of course, U.S.G.S. maps may be oriented in the same way. This time:

1. Place compass on map so that compass north-south coincides with any map meridian. (Some maps show one or more meridians or at least tick marks at top and bottom to represent them. If none are shown, right and left margins probably are aligned with True North.)
2. Rotate map (simultaneously with compass) until meridian and compass needle are separated by the number of degrees in the declination. Make

certain that the needle is on the correct side of True North.

Identification of ground detail is a matter of comparing map bearings with field bearings. Once the map is oriented in good view of the features one wants to identify, the two bearings are really the same thing and are taken at the same time:

1. Orient the map.
2. Determine the party's position on the map.
3. Place compass on or directly behind map position and sight (or point DOT arrow) toward unidentified ground feature (*Figure 10*).

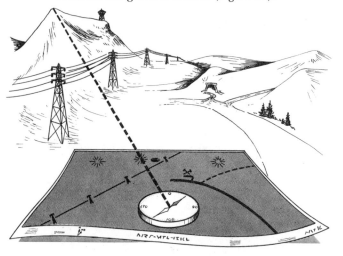

Figure 10. Once the map is properly oriented, map and field bearings are one and the same. Ground features may then be identified along the common bearing.

4. If feature is shown on map, it will be found along the bearing.

Caution: Examine all features along the bearing for elevation. A relatively low ridge in the foreground can block the view of a much higher one a greater distance away.

The Back Bearing

The back bearing is a return compass direction. In the field it is obtained by taking a backsight on some landmark along the rear extension of the point-line. Do not wait until the return trip to establish identifiable return landmarks.

For map work, the TYPE A compass is a perfect computer of back bearings because the two ends of its needle always point to reciprocal pairs of readings on the card. After writing down the forward bearing, turn the compass until either end of the needle is on the new reading. The other end will be on the degree value of the back bearing. Orientation does not matter because the needle is only being used as a divider.

Without the mechanical help of the needle, the reciprocal of any compass reading may be found by adding or subtracting 180°. Here is the rule:

If the forward reading is *less* than 180°, add 180° to it.

If the forward reading is *more* than 180°, subtract 180°.

If you can't remember which is which, think of it this way. Doing the wrong thing will give an answer of less than 0° or more than 360°, and both of these of course are nonsense.

Be careful not to confuse forward and back bearings. A route sketch is an invaluable idea because it puts route segments and compass directions into graphic order. As readings are taken and recorded, put them on the route sketch with some notation to show direction. Let's try this with an example.

Suppose that the forward bearing just read is 247°, and that you wish to compute the back bearing.

1. Turn the compass housing until one end of the needle is on 247°.
2. Read the other end of the needle. It will be on 67°.
3. Record them on the route sketch as 247° → and 67° ←.
4. Choose a landmark along the back bearing.

Either way the back bearing is obtained, in the field or from the map, frequent checking will be necessary as the party actually progresses along the route. It may also be necessary to alter it if no good landmark appears along its line or close to it. As soon as the route changes markedly a new back bearing must be established.

At this point in his reading, the owner of a TYPE A compass should skip to Chapter 5.

3 / The Type B Compass

Check your compass once again to see that it fits this description:

Any compass in which the compass card and the compass needle are joined and work as a unit.

Many compasses of this design in use today are of the military (lensatic) type. Some of these have been declared surplus by the government in past years and many more have been manufactured "surplus" for the outdoor market. This chapter is written primarily with the lensatic model in mind. There are also a number of models on the market which fit the description above but which do not have the lens or special sighting arrangement. The same directions apply to these although they are basically simpler than the lensatic model and will require less comment.

Figure 11. The TYPE B compass. This is the military lensatic model. Note the lens on the raised tab and the sighting notches on the tab and front of cover.

The lens in the lensatic system is a small magnifying glass mounted on a hinged tab (*Figure 11*). The glass can be raised to a point where the user is able to see a magnified reading while sighting toward an objective. The front sight of the compass is a fine wire centered in a slit in the compass housing cover. This front sight can be used in a vertical position for field work or in a horizontal position for lining up points on a map.

The line formed by the wire and sights is frequently called a lubber's line. In the early days of sailing, when the magnetic compass was the only navigational aid of importance, a line was painted on the deck down the center axis of the ship. It passed directly through the wheel house and the steersman used it exactly as we shall, as a reference mark from which to measure the angle between north and the direction of travel.

If your TYPE B is not a lensatic model it will probably have some kind of a lubber's line anyway. It may be a line on the glass housing cover or an "N" marked on the rim of the housing itself. If you find none, then you should make a reference mark by scratching or painting a line on the housing. It can be at any point on the rim so long as it forms a line with the center pivot when sighted toward an objective. The exact place does not matter because the housing of the TYPE B, except for this mark, has no part in the reading of the compass; that is, the compass card is not fixed to the housing and the housing itself has no scales or arrows which assist in the reading. The only function of the reference mark, like the sighting line of the lensatic compass, is to make it easier to sight across a given reading or to sight on a particular objective.

The lens-sight arrangement of the lensatic compass is capable of improving the accuracy of sightings; however, it will soon be discovered that any increase in accuracy will depend on the navigator's ability to hold the compass steady during the sighting and reading. The correct sighting position for the lensatic compass is shown in *Figure 12*.

Figure 12. Proper way to take sighting position with the lensatic compass. Note the thumb brace (beneath the lens tab) and the pistol grip effect it gives the hands.

Most Type B compasses have no damping device to control the oscillations of the compass needle, but there are a couple of ways to get around the problem. As the compass needle and card swing, Magnetic North is always at the midpoint of the described arc. The sharp-eyed navigator can note the extremes of the swing and mentally halve the distance. For example, the midpoint of an arc between 10° and 30° is of course at 20°. The oscillations can also be checked by tilting the compass just as the needle reaches the approximate midpoint of one of its swings. This will ground the compass card against the housing. When released (by the compass being made level again) the needle-and-card assembly will probably continue to swing, but in a much smaller arc. The checking process may be repeated until oscillations are short enough to be waited out or else ignored.

In wilderness travel, any accuracy that can be gained with a refined sighting arrangement is probably canceled out by problems which are inherent in compass navigation. We hasten to add, however, that it never hurts to start out as much on course as possible. A 3° error in the reading, coupled with a probable similar error in following the course, adds up to a sizable miss after only a short distance. Besides, accuracy is part of the challenge and enjoyment of wilderness navigating.

The TYPE B compass is designed to give *magnetic* readings only. These must be converted to True values in order to use them in the field and to relate them to map bearings, guidebook descriptions, or perhaps the navigator's own previous notes.

Any compass can be used to navigate by magnetic bearings alone. The TYPE B is particularly well suited to this approach.* The system, however, is confusing when used with maps, which invariably are drawn in True orientation. In addition, when bearings are given in some written source, they almost always are given in True form. Consequently, the student who intends to learn the compass thoroughly will realize that he must know how to make conversions anyway. When he does know his craft well he will also know when he may use magnetic readings and when he must convert them to True form. For now, the simpler system is the one which works in all situations.

---

* A section in the Appendix entitled Simplified Compass Navigation outlines the method, but beware the "simplification."

Reading TYPE B

Reading the compass is essentially the process of associating a degree value on the compass card with a particular ground direction. There are two field situations, just the reverse of one another, in which this is done: *taking* a bearing on a known objective; and *using* a (known) bearing to locate an unknown objective. Both situations are concerned with lining up the same three points, the difference being in which one of them is unknown. These three points, which we shall refer to as the *point-line* are:

1. The navigator's starting position. (This is not map position, but simply where he stands. It is always "known.")
2. The reading on the compass card.
3. The objective.

Point-lines for the separate field situations of taking and using bearings are shown in *Figures 13* and *14*.

The card of the TYPE B compass, because it is attached to the magnetic needle, always maintains a Magnetic North orientation. Any bearing sighted with it is a magnetic bearing. To obtain True direction the navigator must consider the amount and direction of magnetic declination for his area of operation. The procedure for taking east declination into account is exactly the opposite of that for west declination. To keep confusion to a minimum we shall spell them out individually. You may wish to read only the applicable section below. (The approximate amount and direction of magnetic declination for any area of the United States is suggested in *Figure 6;* however, it will be more accurately given on local U.S.G.S. topographic maps.)

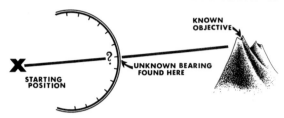

Figure 13. The point-line for *taking* a bearing with a TYPE B compass.

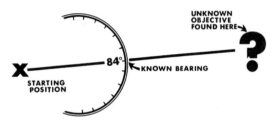

Figure 14. The point-line for *applying* a bearing with a TYPE B compass. Whether taking a bearing or using a predetermined one, the point-line is made up of the same three points. Two known quantities help to locate an unknown one. With TYPE B the magnetic declination will also have to be considered.

East Declination

Let us work with a sample declination of 22° east, which happens to be that for the Seattle, Washington, area. With the needle declining 22° to the right (east) of True North, the navigator must think in terms of

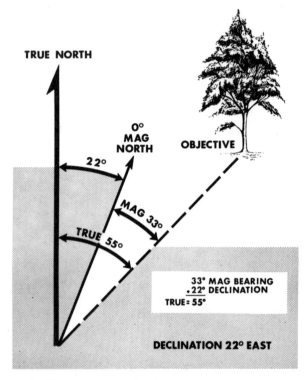

TRUE NORTH

0°
MAG
NORTH

OBJECTIVE

22°

MAG 33°

TRUE 55°

33° MAG BEARING
+22° DECLINATION
TRUE= 55°

DECLINATION 22° EAST

Figure 15. East declination must be *added* to a magnetic bearing to obtain True direction.

the numbers on his compass card as lagging 22° behind True bearings at all times. Study *Figure 15* carefully.

To change any magnetic bearing to a True bearing, east declination (the laggard degrees) must be *added* in. If the conversion is from True back to magnetic form, the east declination will then have to be *subtracted* out. Remember the rule one way—"Mag to True; Add East"—when taking a bearing and the

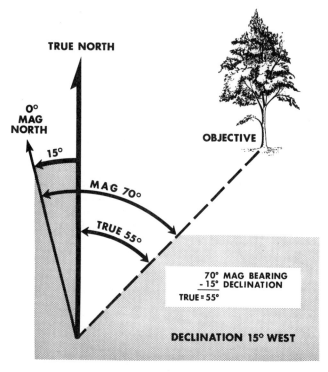

TRUE NORTH

0°
**MAG
NORTH**

15°

MAG 70°

TRUE 55°

OBJECTIVE

70° MAG BEARING
- 15° DECLINATION
TRUE = 55°

DECLINATION 15° WEST

Figure 16. West declination must be *subtracted* from a magnetic bearing to obtain True direction.

alternative, for putting the bearing back into the magnetic form the compass works with, will come to mind automatically—"True to Mag; Subtract East."

West Declination

Let us work with a sample declination of 15° west, which runs through New England from the northwest corner of Vermont to Cape Cod, Massachusetts.

With the needle declining 15° to the left (west) of True North, the navigator must think in terms of the numbers on his compass card as being 15° *ahead* of True North at all times. Study *Figure 16* very carefully.

To change any magnetic bearing to a True bearing, west declination (the eager degrees) must be *subtracted* out. If the conversion is from True back to magnetic form, the west declination will then have to be *added* back in. Remember the rule one way — "Mag to True; Subtract West" — when taking a bearing, and the alternative, for putting the bearing back into the magnetic form, will come to mind automatically: "True to Mag; Add West."

The Type B Compass in the Field

Here are the individual steps for taking and using bearings in the field:

Field Situation #1: Taking a Bearing

The navigator takes a bearing when he can see the objective and wishes to know its degree value. He must:

1. Face the objective.
2. Sight along the center pivot and across the reference mark (or along the lensatic sights) toward the objective.
3. Read the magnetic bearing where the sighting line crosses the compass card.
4. "Add East" or "Subtract West" declination.

The result of taking a bearing and converting it to True form is a bearing ready for relating to maps, guidebooks, or route descriptions, and your own previous route-finding notes. *Write it down!* Tired feet or carefree souls are poor memory aids.

Field Situation #2: Using a Bearing

The navigator uses a bearing from a given source — a map*, a guidebook, or his own previous notes — when he cannot locate the objective by sight. He must:

1. *Reverse* the declination rule. (It now becomes "Subtract East" and "Add West.")
2. Rotate the compass until the sights line up with the magnetic bearing on the card.
3. Choose an identifiable landmark along the bearing. It will be the objective for one segment of the route.

There is of course a third field situation which occurs when the navigator cannot see his objective and has no given bearing to follow either. This becomes a matter of compass technique rather than of reading and will be covered later.

Orienting a Map for Field Use

Before a map can be of use in the field it must be keyed to the earth's true geographic directions. Map detail will then coincide with ground detail and the map can be used to identify significant route and terrain features.

---

* Taking a bearing from a map involves the use of a protractor to measure the angle between True North and the objective, while any compass card is actully a protractor, the pivoting TYPE B card makes a poor one. See Chapter 6, Maps and Map Reading, the section on map direction, for the protractor-straightedge method.

U.S.G.S. topographic maps have a handy declination diagram (or compass rose) which makes map orientation easy. It consists of two lines joined at an angle equaling the magnetic declination for the particular sheet (*see Figure 6*). Use the declination diagram for orienting a map by following these steps:

1. Place the center pivot of the compass at the tip of the declination diagram angle.
2. Rotate the map beneath compass until the compass needle coincides with the line indicating Magnetic North (MN) on the diagram. (The position of the **TYPE** B sighting line does not really matter during map orientation, but it may be used to line up on the diagram's True North line.

When using maps without a declination diagram, work from a map meridian in the same manner. Of course, U.S.G.S. maps may also be oriented in this way. This time:

1. Place compass center pivot directly over a map meridian. (Map margins usually indicate True directions. If so they may be used as meridians.)
2. Rotate map (simultaneously with compass) until meridian and compass needle are separated by the number of degrees in the local declination. Make certain that the needle is on the correct side of True North.

Once oriented to True directions, the map is a mini-model of the earth around you. Identification of a particular ground feature is accomplished by taking a bearing from the party's map position to the feature, then locating the map version of the feature along the bearing (*Figure 17*).

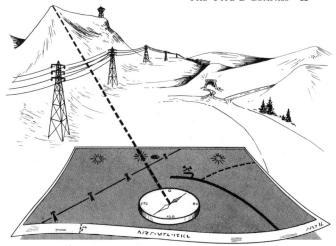

Figure 17. Once the map is properly oriented, map and field bearings are one and the same. Ground features may then be identified along the common bearing.

1. Orient the map.
2. Determine the party's map position.
3. Place compass center pivot on or directly behind map position and sight toward unidentified feature
4. If feature is shown on map, it will be found along the line of sight. (There is no need to take a particular reading if identification is the only purpose.)

Caution: Examine all features along the bearing for elevation. A relatively low ridge in the foreground can block the view of a much higher one a greater distance away.

The Back Bearing

The back bearing is a return compass direction. In the field it is obtained by taking a backsight on some landmark along the rear extension of the point-line. Do not wait until the return trip to establish identifiable return landmarks and back bearings.

For map work, the back bearing will be the reciprocal of the forward reading, and directly opposite on the compass card. There is no need to make a separate measurement to find it. To find the reciprocal of any bearing, apply the following rule:

• If the forward bearing is *less* than 180°, *add* 180° to it to obtain the back bearing.

• If the forward bearing is *more* than 180°, *subtract* 180° from it to obtain the back bearing.

If there should be any problem in remembering which is which, think of it this way. Doing the wrong thing will result in an answer of either less than 0° or more than 360°, both of which are nonsense.

Be careful not to confuse forward and back bearings. A route sketch is an invaluable idea because it puts route segments and compass directions into graphic order.

Either way the back bearing is obtained — by taking a reading in the field, or by finding the reciprocal of the map bearing — frequent checking will be necessary as the party progresses along its route. It may also be necessary to alter the back bearing in the field if no suitable landmark can be found along its line. As soon as the route changes direction a new back bearing must be established.

At this point in his reading, the owner of a TYPE B compass should skip to Chapter 6, Maps and Map Reading.

4 / *The*
Type C
Compass

Check your compass once again to be certain that it fits this description:

The Type C compass is any compass with a *counterclockwise* numbering system.

The Forester compass, the major Type C in wide use, takes its name from the fact that it is of the design and caliber used by professional people whose work takes them into the outdoors — surveyors, geologists, forestry workers. Another name for the design is Cruiser, from the job of "cruising" a stand of timber to estimate its value.

The instrument almost fits the description of the Type A compass given in the glossary, but among its many distinctive features is one which puts it into a category by itself. That is its *reversed* degree numbering system. The compass *is read at the north-indicating tip of the needle.* As it is usually designed, the instrument has at least two and sometimes three numbering systems, each to be used separately. These make it truly versatile even if slightly bewildering at first. We will mention two of these scales in passing, but our major concern will be the reversed azimuth scale.

Figure 18 shows the conventional azimuth compass card on the floor of the housing. It serves as a useful reminder of the orientation of True east and west (for they are reversed on the outer dial we shall be using). If used with this card alone the Forester-Cruiser is no different from a TYPE A compass.

Around the outside of the conventional azimuth card is a raised dial which carries two more number-

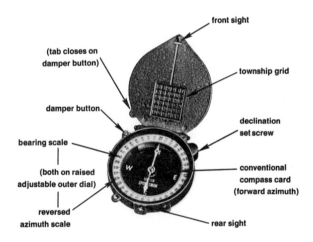

Figure 18. The TYPE C compass, often called the Forester or Cruiser compass.

ing scales. The inner set of numbers is the quadrant or Bearing scale. Because it can be used with any compass, the Bearing system is described in the Appendix. The outer set of numbers is the reversed azimuth scale with which we shall be concerned. We will come back to it after a look at the general characteristics of the Forester compass.

The Forester is designed for accuracy which comes close to rough survey work. The better models are durable, highly versatile, and easy to operate, making them one of the better instruments for serious route-finding.

Several design features contribute to its accuracy and ease of operation. One is a device which allows the raised dial inside the housing to be adjusted right or left for east or west declination. After setting the dial for a given locale, magnetic declination can very nearly be ignored; the compass will yield True directions. Another advantage is the mechanical damper with which the oscillations of the needle may be controlled. On most models the cover closes down on the damper button, locking the needle in place when the compass is not in use. This saves needless wear on the needle-center pivot assembly as the instrument is carted about in pockets or packs. A third feature, which some say facilitates the taking of finer readings, is the closely calibrated dial.* Tickmarks are one degree apart and the needle has a sharp point for good accuracy. Taking full advantage of this, however, requires a tripod or at least a firm stand of some type.

---

*This is a debatable point. The author feels that tickmarks of at least 2° spacing are easier to read. The eye easily splits that distance, even a 5° space, when necessary.

Rifle-type sights mounted near the "S" mark on the housing and at the tip of the open front cover are designed to pinpoint compass sightings. The sighting line can be seen down the center of the cover in *Figure 18*. Also on the cover is a numbered grid which represents the numbering sequence of the sections of land under the township surveying system. A township is a six-miles-square plot of land containing thirty-six sections of land, each of one square mile. All but the thirteen original states and Kentucky, Maine, Tennessee, Texas, Vermont, and West Virginia are surveyed with this system. In most other areas then, the markers which locate the corners of sections can be used in determining direction and distance.*

Several times we have mentioned accuracy in connection with the Forester compass. The usual nature of wilderness terrain makes it difficult to obtain better than 2° degrees of accuracy in a route of any length no matter how accurate the sighting and reading of the compass. The point should be made, however, that it is far better to start out on the beam than to compound inevitable navigational problems with poor sighting habits. An error of 5° or 6° can cause you to miss a very large target after only a couple of miles. For many wilderness navigators, accuracy is part of the fun of the sport anyway.

Adjusting TYPE C for Magnetic Declination

In Chapter 1 we learned that the magnetic needle declines from True North by a given amount and

---

*For an informative treatment, in lay terms, of the township system in wilderness navigating, see *Map, Compass, and Campfire;* Binfords & Mort, publishers; by Donald E. Ratliff.

direction. Both of these factors depend on where in North America the user is located. A declination, for example, of 5° east means that Magnetic North is located in a True direction 5° to the east of True North. In order to adjust the compass for this declination, its dial must be turned until the 5° tickmark appears along the sighting line. Because the Forester is read at the tip of the needle, needle and sighting line will be in alignment when the compass is sighted toward Magnetic North. Any other sighted direction will also be a True direction, read at the needle tip, because the dial will have been rotated 5° in the proper direction to account for the declination in the reading.

Here is how to adjust TYPE C for any declination: rotate the outer dial, by means of the adjusting screw (*Figure 18*) until the degree value of the declination appears along the sighting line. The tickmark at N on the compass housing floor is a handy reference mark for this adjustment. It falls along the sighting line and of course is not moved during the adjustment.

Examples:

22° east declination

Turn the dial to the right until the 22° tickmark appears on the sighting line.

15° west declination

Turn the dial to the *left* until 345° (360° minus 15° declination) appears on the sighting line.

Reading a TYPE C Compass

Reading the compass is the process of associating one of its degree values with a particular ground direction. This occurs in two field situations: *taking* a bearing on a known objective, and *using* a bearing to locate an unknown objective. Both of these are concerned with lining up the same three points, the difference being in which of the three is unknown. The points, which we shall refer to as the *point-line*, are:

1. The navigator's starting position. (This is not map position, but simply where he stands. It is always "known.")
2. The reading on the compass card. (With TYPE C, actually a bit off the point-line proper.)
3. The objective.

Point-lines for the separate field situations of taking and using bearings are shown in *Figures 19* and *20*. Here are the steps in each case:

Field Situation #1: Taking a Bearing

The navigator takes a bearing when he can see the objective and wishes to know its degree value. He must:

1. Face the objective.
2. Sight along the sighting line toward it.
3. Use the damper device to steady the needle.
4. Read the bearing at the north indicating end of needle.

   Write it down! Tired feet and carefree souls make poor memory aids.

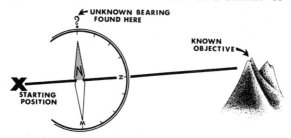

Figure 19. The point-line for *taking* a bearing with a TYPE C compass.

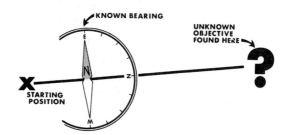

Figure 20. The point-line for *applying* a bearing with a TYPE C compass. Whether taking or using a bearing, the point-line is made up of the same three points. In each case two known quantities help to locate a third unknown one. Note that with TYPE C one of the "points" is not actually on the line.

Field Situation #2: Using a Bearing

The navigator uses a bearing from a map, a guide-book, or from his own previous notes, to locate an objective which he cannot see or identify. He must:

1. Rotate the compass until the bearing appears at the north-indicating tip of the needle.
2. Sight along the sighting line and choose an objective toward which to navigate.

There is of course a third situation which occurs when the navigator has no predetermined bearing and cannot see his objective either. This is more a matter of technique than of reading the compass as such, and will be taken up in a later chapter. Another compass use, that of taking a bearing from a map, uses the compass card as a protractor and does not employ the magnetic principles of the compass itself. The process is the same for any instrument so is explained in Chapter 6, Maps and Map Reading, in the section on map direction.

The logic of the TYPE C design is beautifully simple —that is, once it is understood! At first it seems overwhelmingly strange that True directions can be read at all from a compass card that has things all backwards. The answer is found in these two factors:

1. The compass is read at a *stationary* point. (The needle tip is "stationary" on Magnetic North.)
2. The numbers on the compass card move past the needle as the housing is rotated to a sighting postion.

Picture what happens when the compass is rotated to a sighting on due east at 90°. To make it simple, assume that the navigator is facing due north to begin with. As he slowly turns himself and his compass to the right, the *left-reading* numbers on the outer dial will be increasing as they parade past the needle. When "90°" and "E" appear at the tip of the needle, the sighting line will be pointing east.

Orienting a Map for Field Use

Before a map can be of use in the field, it must be keyed to the earth's geographic or true directions. Map detail will then coincide with ground detail and the map can be used to identify significant route features.

U.S.G.S. topographic maps have a handy declination diagram (or compass rose) which makes map orientation easy. It consists of two lines joined at an angle equaling the magnetic declination for the particular sheet. Use the declination diagram for orienting a map by following these steps:

1. Place compass center pivot on point of declination diagram angle.
2. Rotate *compass* until its north-south line—for TYPE C this is the 0°-180° line in the azimuth scale on the floor of the housing—coincides with the diagram's True North line.
3. Rotate *map* (simultaneously with compass) until compass needle coincides with the diagram's Magnetic North (MN) line.

When using maps without a declination diagram, work from a map meridian in the same manner. Of course, U.S.G.S. maps may also be oriented in this way. This time:

1. Place compass on map so that compass north-south (again using the scale on the housing floor) coincides with any map meridian. Right and left map margins usually are aligned to map north, and if so may be used as meridians.
2. Rotate map (simultaneously with compass) until meridian and compass needle are separated by the number of degrees in the local declination. Make certain that the needle is on the correct side of True North.

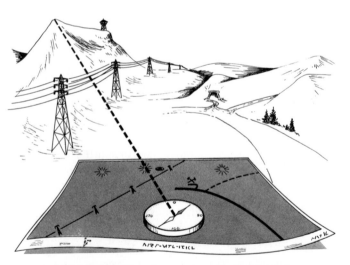

Figure 21. Once the map is properly oriented, map and field bearings are one and the same. Ground features may then be identified along the common bearing.

Identification of ground detail is a matter of comparing map bearings with field bearings. Once the map is oriented in good view of the features one wants to identify, the two bearings are really the same thing and are taken at the same time:

1. Orient the map.
2. Determine the party's position on the map.*
3. Place the compass on or directly behind established map position and in line with the unidentified ground feature.
4. If the feature is shown on the map it will be found along this line of sight. (There is no need to take a particular reading if identification is the only purpose.)

Caution: Examine all features along the bearing for elevation. A relatively low ridge in the foreground can block the view of a much higher one a greater distance away.

The Back Bearing

The back bearing is a return compass direction. In the field it is obtained by taking a backsight on some landmark along the rear extension of the point-line. Do not wait until the return trip to establish identifiable return landmarks.

For map work, the TYPE C compass is a perfect computer of back bearings because the two ends of its needle always point to reciprocal pairs of readings on the compass card. After writing down the forward bearing, turn the compass card until either end of

---

* See Chapter 9, Knowing Where You Are.

the needle is on the new reading. The other end will be on the degree value of the back bearing. Orientation does not matter because the needle is only being used as a divider.

Without the mechanical help of the needle, the reciprocal of any compass reading may be found by adding or subtracting 180°. Here is the rule:

- If the forward reading is *less* than 180°, *add* 180° to it.
- If the forward reading is *more* than 180°, *subtract* 180° from it.

If you can't remember which is which, think of it this way. Doing the wrong thing will result in an answer of less than 0° or more than 360°. Either of these of course is nonsense.

Be careful not to confuse forward and back bearings. A route sketch is an invaluable idea because it puts route segments and compass directions into graphic order. As readings are taken and recorded, put them on the route sketch with some notation to show direction—for example, the reciprocals of 247°→ and 67°←, whose arrows denote the forward and the return directions respectively.

Either way the back bearing is obtained, in the field or from the map, frequent checking will be necessary as the party actually progresses along the route. It may also be necessary to alter it if no good landmark appears along its line or close to it. As soon as the route changes markedly a new back bearing must be established.

5 / *A Deeper Look at Magnetic Declination*

In this chapter, in order to give a better understanding of the seemingly whimsical nature of magnetic declination, we shall take up a bit of the how and why of the earth's magnetism.

Though magnetic power is invisible, its *lines of force* can easily be demonstrated. Iron filings sprinkled over a piece of paper held above an ordinary bar magnet will align themselves in a pattern as shown in *Figure 22*. These *lines of force* flowing from pole to pole of the magnet are identical in principle to the larger system within and over the earth, for the earth itself acts like a huge bar magnet.

The compass needle aligns itself with the earth's lines of force exactly as does a tiny iron filing in its smaller system. Man has induced more permanent

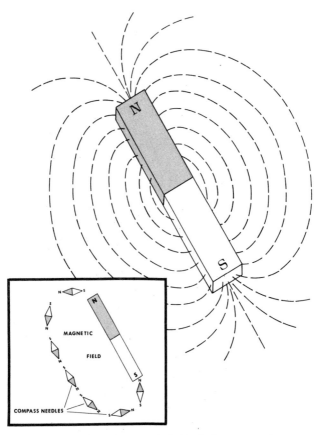

Figure 22. The magnetic field of a bar magnet is an uncomplicated miniature version of the magnetic field of the earth. The inset illustrates how a compass needle aligns itself with the lines of force within a magnetic field.

magnetism into the compass needle to improve upon the small traces which are present in most iron. This, along with a pivot to reduce friction, allows the needle to maintain a magnetic orientation. The compass circle or card completes the picture by giving the needle something to be oriented to.

As *Figure 23* suggests, the earth's magnetic lines of force are not nearly so well defined as those about the bar magnet. With many deviating influences at

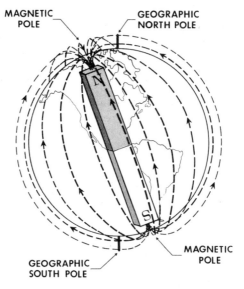

MAGNETIC POLE

GEOGRAPHIC NORTH POLE

MAGNETIC POLE

GEOGRAPHIC SOUTH POLE

Figure 23. This drawing is suggestive only. The magnetic field of the earth is very much like that of a bar magnet, though vastly more complex. Neither, in fact, is completely understood by scientists as yet.

work they seem to swirl in odd patterns over and around the earth. Its lines are also subject to many types of changes in pattern; though most are inconsequential for compass work, it is well to be aware of them. The amazing order in nature can be amazingly disorderly at times, and no one entering a wilderness can afford to do so with the notion that "natural" is always filed under "N," or in this case, that a declination of X° east will be just that because it is printed on the map.

The earth's lines of force are subject to more or less predictable changes during periods of increased or decreased solar activity (called magnetic storms or sun spots) and to decidedly less predictable changes during locally poor weather conditions, especially during thunder storms. Other permanent variations exist due to differences in the composition of the earth's crust, and possibly even due to the alterations man himself has made in and on the surface of the earth. Changes are of two natures: some are cyclical, while others return to "normal" only with the conditions which brought them on.

There is another change in declination which is of greater importance because it is in one direction only, irreversible, and of significant proportions over a few years' time. It is known as *annual westward change*.

The entire magnetic field of the earth, virtually intact, changes position with respect to the surface of the earth. The most commonly accepted theory of why this is so is a rather fascinating one. The earth's magnetic field is thought to be generated by the flow of materials in its liquid center. At least its lines of force and magnetic poles are associated with its center rather than its more stable crust. As the earth rotates *eastward* on its axis, some slight slippage *westward* of its liquid center is believed to take place.

The whole thing can be likened to a pail of water rotated with a constant motion. Physical law states that "bodies at rest tend to remain at rest"; in other words, that both water and pail (or liquid center and crust) will tend to resist the rotational force, and the water will be more successful than the rigid container. Anyone who has ever carried a bucket of water knows how easy it is to spin the container without greatly disturbing the contents. With a constant rotational force in one direction, friction between water and pail will cause the water's speed to *almost* equal that of the pail, though an observable point on the water's surface, such as a chip of wood, might be seen to slip backward over a period of time.

If we accept the possibility that the earth's magnetic field is related to flowing currents within its liquid center, it is easy to visualize what must take place regarding declination change. As the earth rotates *eastward* (think of it as turning toward the sunrise) its entire magnetic field, lines of force and all, will be slipping *westward* by some amount equal to the slippage of the earth's liquid center. This is exactly what appears to be taking place.

Annual Westward Change

Whether the "slippage" theory is correct or not, the observed annual change is fact. To keep topographic maps current without having to reprint them frequently, the U.S.G.S. and other mapping agencies date the declination diagram on each sheet. Along with the date should be a declination change factor.

For example:

> Approximate mean declination 1950.
>
> Annual westward change 7' (minutes).

In order to update his declination information from 1950 to, say, 1972 the owner of that particular map must multiply twenty-two years times the change factor of 7'. This yields 2° 34' of total change which must (in this case) be subtracted from the shown declination.* To understand the mechanics of the change pick a city or location somewhere on the chart in *Figure 6* and imagine holding it down with your foot while shoving the isogonic lines westward. The effect would be to drag a more easterly value to the spot you have chosen. If it is in an area of west declination, that value will be a higher one; if it is in an area of east declination, the value will be lower; or, if your "foot" was close to the agonic line, you just might have changed the declination from east to west.

The declination change factor in the above example was taken from a map with a 5° east declination. Its declination now is closer to 2°, and before too many years the area will be on the agonic 0° line and start the change to a west declination. You will note that the isogonic lines in *Figure 6* are much closer together in that area than they are, for example, on the West coast. Seattle, Washington, had a declination of about 23° in the 1950s, yet, approaching the 1970s, its declination was more correctly 22°.

Do not be confused between the direction of declination and the direction of its annual change. Declination refers to the angle between True North and Magnetic North from where you stand with your compass. The annual change is always westward, and

---

* 22 years × 7' = 154' $\dfrac{154'}{60' \text{ per degree}}$ = 2° 34'

it involves the entire magnetic field of the earth.

One important concept remains to be clarified regarding lines of force and declination. The lines shown in declination charts such as *Figure 6* are *not* magnetic lines of force representing the earth's magnetic field. The compass needle will not necessarily point in the direction of the line on the chart. (It may, coincidentally.) The lines on the chart are "isogonic" lines, meaning lines of equal angle; at all points along one particular line the angle between the compass needle and True North will be the same.

If an observer could walk one of these isogonic lines, say the line of 22° east declination which passes through Seattle, his travels in the U.S. would start near Point Barrow, Alaska, thousands of miles *north* of Seattle. He would progress due south through the state to Kodiak Island, swing gradually south-east then east over the Pacific, then more northeasterly through Seattle and Washington state before going almost due north again through Canada toward the magnetic pole. In spite of the many changes of direction and in spite of the many different *actual* angles between geographic and magnetic polar areas, his compass would always read 22°.

The one line on the declination chart of 0° is an "agonic" line, the prefix "a-" meaning "no." It is the line along which there is no angle between Magnetic and True Norths.

An interesting and up-to-date chart of magnetic declination and annual westward change is available for fifty cents from:

The U.S. Dept. of Commerce
Coast and Geodetic Survey
Distribution Division C44
Washington, D.C. 20235

Ask for "Isogonic Chart of the U.S. No. 3077." The chart also shows significant local deviations in magnetic declination in much more detail than is possible to show in *Figure 6*.

Declination and Deviation

Any magnetic influence on the compass needle which is not due to the earth's "regular" magnetic field is called magnetic *deviation*. It is also called *variation* and *local attraction,* but all three names convey the same sense of an extra or irregular source. These sources, ranging from natural ore deposits to the hunter's rifle barrel, will cause the compass needle to indicate a reading which is over or under that of the supposed declination for the area.

Fortunately for navigation all magnetic forces work according to a mathematical law which describes their rapidly lessening effect with distance from the compass.* A magnet placed next to a compass will have a strong effect on the compass needle; however, when the magnet is moved two feet away its affect will be *four* times less. When moved three feet away its affect will be *nine* times less, and so on. In application, this means that a pocket knife in the hand may greatly affect the compass needle, while in the pocket it may not affect it at all. A paper clip held next to the compass will move the needle several degrees, but an automobile a few yards away will hardly change the reading, if at all. Auto and aircraft

---

* This is the law of inverse squares. It states that the amount of influence is inversely proportional to the square of the distance between the compass needle and the source of magnetic force. "Inverse" means that as the distance becomes larger, the force becomes smaller.

compasses have small, built-in, adjustable magnets which can be set to counteract far larger and stronger magnetic influences just a few feet away. Such tiny compensating magnets can and do effectively neutralize the extraneous magnetism in an entire aircraft carrier.

For practical navigational purposes there is little difference between declination and deviation. In a literal sense, declination is the total amount by which the needle declines away from True North, however, there must be some way to tell how much of the decline is due to regular sources, which can be found on the chart or on maps, and how much is due to erratic and irregular sources. Deviation is often unsuspected.

Pocket knives, ice axes, cameras, etc., if they are responsible at all, will usually have such a dramatic affect that their detection should not take long. Natural ore deposits, transmission lines, railroad tracks, etc., can have a more subtle effect, and for this reason a method other than detection by hunch must be employed.

The stars, Polaris in particular in the Northern Hemisphere, provide us with a method of checking on the total of declination *plus deviation.*

Checking On Deviation

Polaris, also called the North Star, is so directly over the earth's north geographic pole that it changes its position but slightly as the earth rotates beneath the night sky. All other stars visibly cross the heavens in curved paths from east to west, just as do the sun and the moon. Stars relatively close to Polaris make small full circles to our view each night, while those more distant make larger circles which causes them to rise and set on the horizons.

Though not a very bright star, Polaris is easily located by two prominent pointer stars in the pan of the Big Dipper (*Figure 24*). The pointers are the two stars which form the front wall of the pan, the side away from the handle of the dipper. They point from

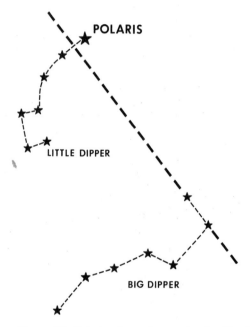

Figure 24. Polaris, the pole star in the Northern Hemisphere, may be located by the pointer stars in the pan of the Big Dipper.

dipper bottom to top. If we consider the distance between the two pointers as one unit, Polaris is located about six units away and very nearly in line with them. There are no other stars in the immediate vicinity which are brighter than the pole star. As a double check, try to locate the Little Dipper as well. Polaris is the last star in the handle of the Little Dipper. The pan bottom of this constellation often appears V-shaped because one of its stars is quite faint. This will be especially true when viewed through city atmospheric conditions.

Type A Compass:

Point 0° directly at the horizon where an imaginary plumb bob from Polaris would touch the ground. Take a reading at the tip of the needle. This angle is the total amount of magnetic influence. If different from the supposed declination, the difference is due to deviation.

Type B Compass:

Sight on Polaris where an imaginary plumb bob would touch the horizon. Take a reading beneath the sighting line or as usual with Type B. The angle between Polaris and Magnetic North is the total magnetic influence at that spot. If different from the expected declination, the difference is deviation.

Type C Compass:

Before adjustment for local declination: Sight on Polaris as above and read the bearing as usual at the tip of the needle. This bearing is the total of declination plus deviation.

After adjustment for local declination: Sight and read the bearing of Polaris in the same manner. If the bearing is 0°, no deviation exists. If other than 0°, the bearing equals the amount of deviation only. The outer dial of the compass must be adjusted until a bearing of 0° is obtained.

Magnetic deviation often has a fickle enough nature to change rapidly over short distances. Erratic readings are one clue to its existence. Under these conditions it is, to say the least, impractical to wait for nightfall and clear skies to prove each reading. It is, however, wise and reassuring, as well as interesting, to make at least one check on deviation while in an unknown area.

The practice of checking both forward and back bearings at *each and every sighting station* may help to reveal local deviation. When deviation exists at one station but not at another, or more strongly at one than the other, the forward and back bearings between the two places will not agree; that is, they will not differ by 180°.

Greater accuracy can be gained with a simple sighting table made by gluing (not tacking) an angle-shaped piece of cardboard to a flat board as in *Figure 25*. The cardboard should be cut on an angle which approximately matches the latitude of the observer.*

---

* Latitude on the earth's surface is represented by a number of degrees from the equator (and counted on "parallels," or imaginary lines, which circle the earth from east to west). It can be found on any map. Interestingly enough, the degree distance of Polaris above the true horizon equals the latitude of the place from which the sighting is made. (The closest thing to a true horizon is a perfectly calm sea.) From the equator (latitude 0°) Polaris makes an angle of 0° with the true horizon; from Minneapolis, nearly astride the 45th parallel, Polaris makes an angle of 45°; and from the north geographic pole Polaris is straight up at 90°.

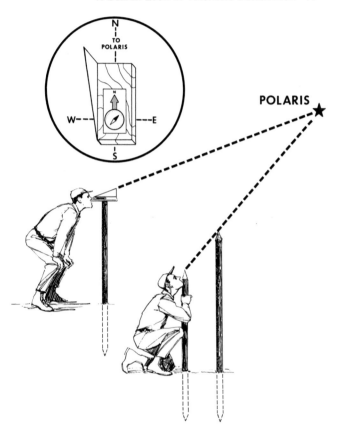

Figure 25. Two methods of checking the compass
needle against True North, represented by
the pole star, to determine the total of expected
declination plus *deviation* due to the possible
extraneous magnetism of a local area.

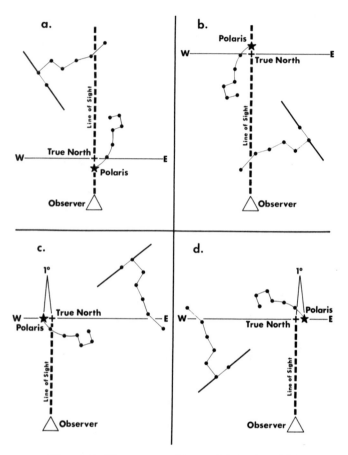

Figure 26. The two positions nightly in which
Polaris is directly aligned with True North
are shown in *a* and *b*. The once nightly position
in which Polaris is 1° west of True North is
shown in *c*, and *d* is the once nightly position
in which it is 1° east of True North. The time
of night these occur changes with the season.

If you live on or near the 35th parallel, cut an angle of 35°, etc. This will allow the compass to sit level on the board, parallel to the cardboard sight, while the sight is aimed directly at Polaris. Utmost care must be taken to free the area of any distracting metals or electrical influences before the sighting is made.

Polaris actually has an apparent rotation of about 2° in diameter, and therefore, twice each night it lines up exactly with True North on the observer's line of sight. As a matter of interest the star may easily be located at the approximate times it best lines up for a declination check. *Figure 26* depicts Polaris in four positions, using the Big and Little Dippers for reference. *Figures a* and *b* show the star when it is directly aligned with True North. *Figures c* and *d* show the star when it is 1° east and west of True North. This 1° may be added to the declination when on the same side of True North, or subtracted from it when declination is on the opposite side. However, with the hand compass such accuracy is far more academic than real.

Polaris has not always been our pole star, nor will it be in the distant future. Two thousand years ago there was no star in close association with True North, but by 1000 A.D. it had moved close enough to be noticed. Today it is only a little more than 1° from being directly over our north geographic pole. Some historians see an important parallel between the development of long-distance navigation and the presence of a dependable marker at True North. At any rate, Polaris has been for centuries an eminent landmark in the sky, and even though we now have more sophisticated navigational aids, the pole star's role has not changed. Every person who steps foot into the wilderness should learn to find it and to know the basic principle it represents. It is an almost permanent compass in the sky.

6

Maps and Map Reading

The world of maps is a fascinating one. There is magic in having a condensed version of the world before the eye. It takes months and even years to put together a good one, though the skillful map reader will continue to find new information for a longer time yet. A map may become outdated when a newer version comes out, but the old one is never useless. With time a map becomes a graphic history of things as they were, and to the user a map is a friend to be treasured and a diary of past adventure.

Like a good book a map is compiled from a great number of sources to give certain kinds of information. It is drawn rather than written but it nevertheless has a definite language composed of lines, colors, and symbols. Happily, it is easier to learn map language than written language. Still, certain basic reading principles should be well understood.

A map is read for four basic kinds of information:

1. Direction
2. Distance
3. Position
4. Identification

These make a good framework from which to approach maps and map reading. Let us take them one at a time.

Direction

Direction implies a reference point. To the right *at 5th Street,* northeast *of here,* and so forth. The common reference point for maps is True North, and map direction is figured in degrees from that point.

Most maps (of the Northern Hemisphere) are drawn with north at the top and south at the bottom, with east and west to the right and left respectively. When no other indication is given, it is a reasonable assumption that map True North is at the top and runs parallel with the margins of the map to True South. More often a map will have both meridians and a compass "rose" to indicate map direction. A meridian is an imaginary line running over the surface of the earth from its True North Pole to its True South Pole. Although the earth can be sliced an infinite number of times with meridians, they will be shown on maps with a spacing of a certain number of degrees convenient for navigation.*

---

* It is impossible *not* to be standing on a meridian. Once the compass user locates True North, he is standing on what navigators call the Observer's Meridian.

A compass rose is a design, usually some form of artful arrow or group of arrows. Its purpose is to indicate cardinal directions on the map. On U.S. Geological Survey maps the compass rose is a pair of lines which form an angle. One line is labeled "N," or marked with an asterisk, to indicate True North, and the other is labeled "MN" for Magnetic North (*See Figure 27*). The angle between them cor-

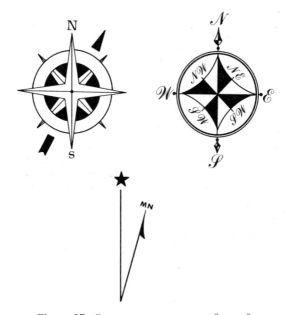

Figure 27. Compass roses range from fancy to functional. The simplest of these three, the bottom design, imparts the most information. It gives True direction and magnetic direction as well. This form is used by the U.S. Geological Survey on topographic maps.

responds to the magnetic declination for that sheet. A third line (creating a second angle) on some sheets will be marked "GN" for grid north. We will not be concerned with it but it is used in a coordinate system of navigation.

Magnetic declination need not be of concern in taking direction from a map. All that is needed is the angle between map True North and the position of the objective on the map. An ordinary protractor—or the compass card, which really is a protractor—will do the job nicely (*Figure 28*). A straightedge of some sort will also be needed, and for this a plain sheet of paper works well. It lies flatter than a ruler and is on the spot for notes and sketches. To obtain a True compass bearing from a map:

1. Connect the starting point to the objective with the straightedge.
2. Place the center mark of the protractor's 0°-180° line along the line created by the straightedge. Rotate the protractor until the same 0°-180° line is parallel to map True North.
3. Read the degree value on the rim of the protractor where it is crossed by the straight edge.

(The compass card is used as a protractor in identical fashion by ignoring the magnetic needle completely. The TYPE B compass cannot be used without orienting the map—to Magnetic North—and making the necessary correction for declination. With TYPE C, use the scale on the floor of the housing since the one on the adjustable outer dial runs counterclockwise.)

It is true that magnetic declination need not be considered in taking a True bearing from a map; how-

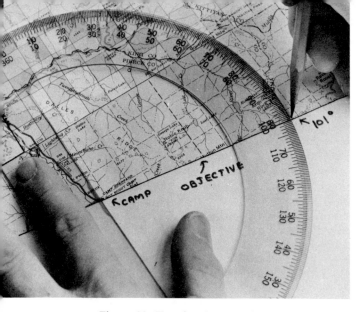

Figure 28. True bearings may be taken from a map with a protractor and straightedge. A sheet of paper works well as a straightedge since it lies flat and is available for notes and sketches.

ever, this is essentially what is done whenever the map is oriented for field use. The major hazard in doing this indoors, where most planning is carried out, lies with stray magnetism or *deviation*. The only house known to the author to be free from nails, screws, electricity and the like is perhaps an igloo. If you live in an igloo, then, or can otherwise be certain that no magnetic deviation is operating, you may take bearings from a map by:

1. Orienting the map with the compass.
2. Placing the center pivot of the oriented compass along a line from starting point to objective.
3. Reading the degree value where the compass card is crossed by the line from start to objective.

79

Note: Be sure to use the declination for the locale of the reading and not necessarily the one shown on the map. Example: If planning an Oregon trip while at home in Chicago, use Chicago's magnetic declination in orienting map and compass.

Some people prefer to draw lines on their maps rather than use a cumbersome straightedge. This is the way it is done in professional navigating, but professionals have access to many copies of the same sheet. It is a personal choice as to whether one wants to muddy up a surface which probably already has more than enough lines on it. With line or straightedge an alternate method is to extend the connection between starting point and objective until it crosses a meridian. Depending on how close to the edge of the map the reading is being taken, the meridian may also have to be extended. Once the intersection is made, the angle can be measured at that point.

The usual problem with putting compass True North-South parallel to a map meridian is that most larger scale maps, the better ones for wilderness navigation, do not show meridians in their entirety. The very popular U.S.G.S. topographic maps use full meridians as side margins, then show tickmarks at top and bottom across the sheet. If a long straightedge is not handy, try making a slight crease. Even the time honored squint-'n-sight method will probably be accurate enough when all other navigational errors are tallied.

Field use of a map is not so arbitrary. When the map is used to identify terrain features or navigational aids it must first be keyed to the earth's True directions. This process of orientation was explained for each major type of compass in Chapters 2, 3, and 4.

Distance

The relationship between map distance and ground distance is the function of scale. Map scale is a measure which expresses the size change undergone by any ground detail which is reduced to fit the paper size of a map. It is usually a pair of numbers in fraction or ratio form that tells the user, in effect, one map unit represents X number of ground units.

A rather far-fetched example will help to clarify what scale is and why it is necessary. If the compiler— the one who assembles all of the information which goes into the map—could use a piece of paper as large as the area being mapped, the map's scale would be 1/1 (or 1:1 in ratio form). One inch of ground would be represented by one inch of map, a one-to-one scale. With the paper only half the size of the map's area of coverage, the scale would be reduced to 1/2. On this map two inches of ground would be represented by the one inch of map space. As the paper becomes smaller, then, scale must also become smaller in order to fit the same ground area onto the paper.

To be manageable the paper size of a map cannot exceed two to three feet in width, and to be useful for wilderness travel the area represented on that paper must be at least a few miles square. Obviously, then, ground detail must be reduced thousands of times to obtain the best combination of paper size and ground area for the type of map being produced. Thus map scale, which tells us how many times the ground area has been reduced, is the determiner of what kind of map is most useful for wilderness travel. In general, the most appropriate scales will run from 1/62500 to 1/20000 and larger.

Map distance, of course, is a direct function of

scale. When a map is compiled, every bit of its detail is placed according to the *pre-chosen* scale. The surveyed distance between selected points in the area of coverage is multiplied by the representative fraction in order to reduce it to map size. All other detail is then placed in the same manner by relating it to these "control" points. In effect, the navigator must reverse the process when taking map distance from the sheet, but most map makers have simplified distance measure by including a *bar scale* in the legend of the map. Such a scale can be seen in *Figure 29*.

The bar scale looks like a small ruler, but be careful not to interpret its divisions as inches, feet, or any other particular unit of measure; each segment of the scale simply tells the user that the same distance on the accompanying map is equal to so many ground units. U.S.G.S. topographic maps usually provide separate bar scales for feet, miles, and kilometers.

Here is one method of using a bar scale to determine map distance:

1. Lay the edge of a sheet of paper along the line between two points of interest and make a pencil mark for each.
2. Transfer the paper to the bar scale and place one mark at zero.
3. Read the scale at the other pencil mark.

Over longer distances, or where the actual route wanders markedly back and forth, greater accuracy can be obtained by dividing the route into approximately straight segments, making a pencil mark for each, then pivoting the paper around to parallel the next one. Try the whole process on the route marked out from Old Mill Bridge to Black Falls in *Figure 29*.

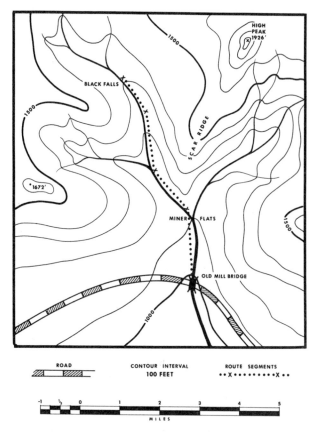

Figure 29. A sample topographic map. We shall refer to this one for examples of drainage and ridge structure, map distance, and contour lines.

The left end of a bar scale is usually more finely divided for determining shorter distances. In *Figure 29*, after finding the Black Falls route to be four plus miles long, slide the last (right-hand) pencil mark back to the "4" mile mark on the scale and read from "0" backwards to see what part of a mile is left over. In this instance it should fall about halfway to the "−1," making a total of about four and one-half miles.

A second very useful way of dealing with map distance involves the number of miles to the inch of map distance at the various scales. This is rather easy to keep in mind because the standard range of map scales is tailor-made to fit the idea. That is, the very popular scale of 1/62500 comes very close to being one mile to the inch, and other scales from there on down (smaller) are multiples of 62,500.*

Here are a few of the more popular map scales and their miles-to-the-inch equivalents:

$$1:20000 = \text{approximately } 1/3 \text{ mile to the inch.}$$
$$1:24000 = \text{approximately } 2/5 \text{ mile to the inch.}$$
$$1:62500 = \text{approximately } 1 \text{ mile to the inch.}$$
$$1:125000 = \text{approximately } 2 \text{ miles to the inch.}$$
$$1:250000 = \text{approximately } 4 \text{ miles to the inch.}$$
$$1:500000 = \text{approximately } 8 \text{ miles to the inch.}$$
$$1:1000000 = \text{approximately } 16 \text{ miles to the inch.}$$

One aspect of scale which troubles people not accustomed to dealing with it is relative size. We might

---

* There are 63,360 inches in a mile. 62,500 inches is only 71 feet 8 inches short of a mile, but the figure is used because it is a common denominator of the standard range of scales. That is, two times 62,500 = 125,000, the denominator of the next smaller widely used scale. Some U.S.G.S. maps of Alaska do use a scale of 1:63360.

be told to obtain large-scale maps for wilderness travel. Well, is 1/24000 large or small?

To begin with, size is relative to use. A jet pilot would find a scale of 1/24000 entirely inadequate. The width of a U.S.G.S. topographic map of that scale represents only about fourteen miles. The aircraft would fly completely over its area of coverage (in under two minutes at 500 m.p.h.) before the pilot could get a bearing on more than a point or two. He would then have to take out the next sheet, which would undoubtedly be useless by the time he got it spread out. This scale is so *large* that only a small land area fits on the map.

On the other hand, a wilderness navigator would find the opposite problem using an aeronautical map with a scale of 1/500000. At this scale there are nearly eight miles to the inch. A man on foot would walk for hours to cover a short map distance, perhaps only one inch in rugged country. Meanwhile he would have little help from the one inch of map. Squeezing 500,000 inches of ground detail into one inch of map does not leave room enough for the amount of detail he needs to identify landmarks. This scale is so *small* that a large land area fits on the map.

We begin to get an inkling about scale size when we examine the representative scale fraction. Take these two, for instance. Which is larger, $\frac{1}{2}$ or $\frac{1}{4}$? The $\frac{1}{2}$ is, of course. Though it has a lesser number in its denominator, the 2 informs us that the whole pie is to be divided only twice, not four times. It is for the same reason that a scale of 1/24000 is larger than a scale of 1/500000. The smaller the denominator, the larger the scale. The top number or numerator is always 1

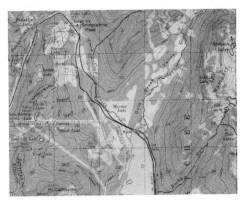

Large scale, 1:62500
U.S. Geological Survey

Small scale, 1:500000
Aeronautical Chart

Medium scale, 1:125000
U.S. Forest Service

Figure 30. Map segments of the same area, approximately four miles square, shown at three different scales.

and it expresses map units. Here is another way to remember the size of scale from the appearance of map
detail:

Small scale means small detail.
Large scale means large detail.

Position

Finding one's position on a map in the usual sense,
such as at the intersection of two compass bearings, is
more a matter of compass technique than of map
reading skill. But there is a second dimension to establishing position which does depend on map reading skill. This is the vertical dimension. On a map it is
referred to as "relief."

Knowledge of the relief of an area is extremely important to a wilderness navigator. But how can he
study the elevation of the land on the flat surface of
a map? Map scale, which helps us to measure all other
distances on a map, is little help. Scale is only responsible for the horizontal placement of map detail.
It can be used to figure the area occupied by a particular relief feature, but it fails relief portrayal where
most important. It makes no distinction between high
and low elevations.

The most graphic technique ever devised to show
relief information is the contour line. Contour lines
are imaginary lines which follow the ground surface
at a constant elevation above sea level. If you were to
walk a contour line you would never go down hill and
never up hill, and eventually you would arrive back
where you started after going completely around the
hill or group of hills in your area. The shoreline of a
lake is a good example of a contour line, though it

goes around the inside of a depression rather than around the outside of a hill. Contour lines do both.

A lake shoreline, in fact, illustrates several important characteristics of contour lines. No matter how long the line is, it always comes back to itself. (The sea level, or "base" contour line, is a case in point. Its line goes around entire continents, which is why it is used as the zero point for measuring elevation.) A second characteristic is that a lake level is always at one and only one elevation at a time. Thirdly, a shoreline, like a contour line on a map, behaves in certain ways according to the kind of terrain features it follows.

Here is a list of other characteristics of contour lines as shown on maps:

• The *contour interval* is the regular elevation difference between all contour lines on a given sheet. It is chosen.

• The *spacing* of contour lines on a given sheet depends on ground slope and map scale. It is not chosen, but is shown to scale.

• Small contour intervals are used on maps with generally flat terrain. Large ones in rugged terrain.

• Index contour lines, every fourth or fifth line, are heavier than others and labeled with elevation figures.

A succession of contour lines, labeled to represent a constant increase or decrease in elevation can very effectively depict both shape and elevation on a flat map. They can also tell us the size and steepness of a particular relief feature. Let's take a look at the logic of contour lines to see how all of this information can come from a set of long swirling lines.

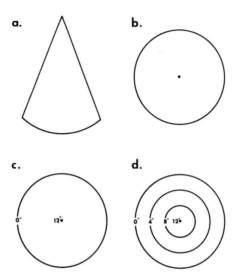

Figure 31. The logic of contour lines is shown in these four drawings. *a.* Side view of a solid cone. *b.* The cone as it would appear on a map. *c.* Elevation figures at base and tip provide a third dimension. *d.* Contour lines reveal shape at regular intervals.

In *Figure 31* are several outline views of an ordinary cone. From the side (*a*) it even looks like a cone. From directly above, though, (*b*), it becomes a dot inside of an ordinary circle. Because we know that it represents a cone, we can easily imagine that the dot marks the top and the circle stands for the base, but so far no relief is actually shown. If, however, we are also told that the cone is twelve inches tall, relief is easily added (*c*) by labeling the lines with elevation figures. Of course, the sides of the figure could be any

shape as it now stands, but that is easily taken care of
(*d*) by adding more circles at regular intervals, say, of
four vertical inches. In the case of our cone the spacing of the circles will also be regular, but only because
a cone's sides slope at a constant rate all the way
around.

In *Figure 32a* the sides are not sloped equally, and
the figure has quite a different appearance when con-
toured. Each line in *32b* still represents only one elevation, but the overhead view causes the lines on the
nearly vertical side to stack up while those on the
other side are even more widely spaced. The chosen
contour *interval* remains at four inches, but the spacing is dictated by the slope of the figure.

With either figure the result is not three dimensional, although with a little practice and some imagi-
nation it can be read as such. The *spacing* of the lines
tells us that the sides of the figure slope at one or
more rates; the shape of the contours tell us the shape
of the figure at selected intervals; and the labels tell us
that the elevation increases (in this case) from outside
to inside.

Now let's put a dip into the rise of what used to be a
perfectly good cone — vary the rate of increase of
slope as in *Figure 33*. Note that as the slope steepens,
contour lines must be more narrowly spaced. The
cone, in fact, is gradually being transformed into a
mountain. Its left side now simulates a protruding
ridge whose contours must bend *outward* in order to
maintain one constant elevation. Its right side simulates a near vertical dropoff or cliff. Question: If this
mountain also had a valley, which way would its contours bend? *Figure 34* adds an extra ridge to Cone
Mountain so that we may see the contours in the

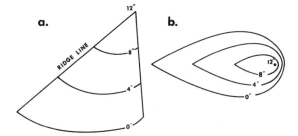

Figure 32. If the left side of the cone in Figure 31 becomes a "ridge" and the right side a near vertical drop (*a*), its map contour lines will show wider and closer spacing (*b*).

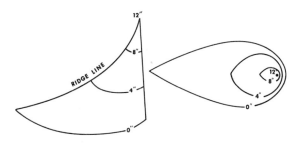

Figure 33. As the sides of a topographical feature change in *rate* of slope, its map contour lines will reflect the rate by changes in spacing.

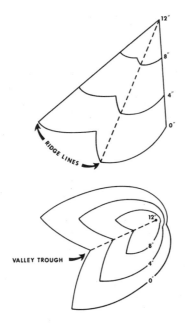

Figure 34. With a second ridge added to the now distorted cone we see a fundamental principle of contour lines: ridge contours point toward the lowlands while valley contours point toward the peaks.

valley formed between them; contours which were bent outward to go around the ridges now must bend inward to define the valley. Actual contours on a topographic map are exceedingly more complex than these examples, but the same elements are there.

At the risk of overstatement, we must emphasize the distinction between the spacing of contour lines and the elevation gain each one represents. The elevation gain or loss, remember, is always the same between any two contour lines for a given map. It is known as the contour interval, or CI, and it will be specified in the map margin, usually near the map scale.

The CI chosen by the compiler will depend largely upon the degree of relief in the area of map coverage. It may be 5, 10, 20, 40, 100, or even 200 feet. It would not do, for example, to use a 100-foot CI on a map where hills did not exceed 150 feet in elevation above the valleys. Conversely, a 5-foot CI in mountainous terrain would force contour lines to be drawn so closely together that they would be unreadable. When a map covers areas of both extremes of relief, the compiler will choose *supplementary* contour lines of intermediate values. These will be labeled and drawn in dashed lines to prevent mistakes.

We do not "see" a map's CI, then, because it is a vertical yardstick. Instead we *count* contour lines and assume each to represent a certain increase or decrease in elevation. In *Figure 29* we can count nine lines from Miner Flats up to the X which marks the summit of High Peak. We know that the last line before the summit is at the 1900 foot level because the CI of the illustration is given as 100 feet. If the X were not labeled, we might correctly assume that the summit lay between the 1900-foot level and the next logical contour at 2000 feet.

While we count lines to determine an elevation gain, we *measure spaces* to determine the distance over which that elevation is gained. Map scale is used exactly as for any other horizontal map distance. Going back to *Figure 29* we note that there are three spaces between Old Mill bridge and Black Falls.

Three times the CI of 100 feet means a vertical rise of 300 feet on the route. In the section on map scale we found that the map distance from bridge to falls over the same route equaled a ground distance of 4.5 miles. Now both figures may be combined to express the average steepness of the route:

$$\text{slope} = \frac{\text{rise}}{\text{distance}}$$

or, changing 4.5 miles to feet,

$$\text{slope} = \frac{300}{23,760} = .013$$

That is a *gradient* of only a little over 1%, a very gentle gain.

After a few experiences of computing slopes and then walking them, you will develop a frame of reference for evaluating the steepness of a route segment from the figures alone. Remember, though, a 90 *degree* slope is 100 *percent*. A 45 *degree* slope is 50 *percent* and so forth.

In the above example the slope was all up hill, but keep in mind that down slopes must be figured separately from rises if you want to keep track of one or the other. On a long backpack it might be interesting to know the total elevation gain or loss. For this it will make no difference whether a portion of the route gains or loses, but, for planning a particular day's trek, it is very important to know how much elevation must be gained in order to reach a planned campsite before darkness falls.

Slope — The Error Factor In Map Distance

Maps are guides to the *horizontal* placement of man-made and natural features on the earth's surface. The vertical nature of these features may be shown by shading, tint bands, contour lines, or spot elevation figures, but such devices do not give us the true ground distance from one elevation to another. Map distance, measured in effect by laying a ruler across the tops of hills, is a crow-flight measure, but we humans must go the up hill and down dale way.

In short, this means that each time a sloped ground distance is measured by way of its portrayal on a flat map, an error will be made. The steeper the slope or the longer the distance, the greater the error will be. To illustrate how it occurs let us build a mountain with perfect dimensions (*Figure 35a*).

Perfect Peak is exactly $1\frac{1}{2}$ miles high — 7,920 feet above sea level, which also happens to be its base. The map shows the distance from the start of the route at the base to the mountain's summit to be one horizontal mile. However, anyone who ventures one mile upward on the resulting 60° slope will find himself only *half* way to the top.* On a slope of 60° then, the error in map distance is exactly 100%.

Examine the triangles in *Figure 35b and 36*. Great geometric detail is not necessary, but it is well to

---

* Mileage for established trails found on trail signs or in printed matter usually is taken from a device which looks like a bicycle wheel attached to wheelbarrow handles. A geared indicator on the wheel does a fair job of recording distance without slope error.

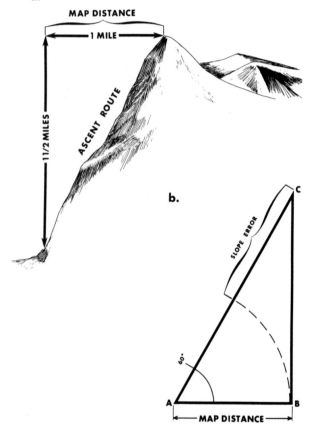

a.

MAP DISTANCE

↤ 1 MILE ↦

ASCENT ROUTE

1 1/2 MILES

b.

C

SLOPE ERROR

60°

A

B

MAP DISTANCE

Figure 35. "Perfect Peak" (*a*) is perhaps an extreme example, but it makes the point that with a 60° slope its ascent route is *twice* as long as its portrayed map distance (*b*).

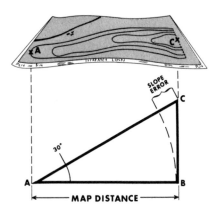

Figure 36. On a 30° slope the slope error amounts to about one-sixth of the shown map distance.

understand the basic logic. The triangles shown are right triangles; that is, they each have one angle of 90°. Considering each of them as a sloped terrain feature, line *AC* corresponds to the walking route to each top. On the other hand, line *AB* – the horizontal distance between base and summit – represents map distance. Line *AC*, the hypotenuse of each right triangle, is always the longer of the two, and the difference between them, *AC* minus *AB*, is the slope error.

Figure 37 portrays the problem in another way by comparing the horizontal placement of two towns on a flat plain with twin peaks on their respective skylines. The map distance between peaks is the same as that between towns, but walking distance over the surface of the earth is another matter. The mountainous route is much longer due to the slopes involved.

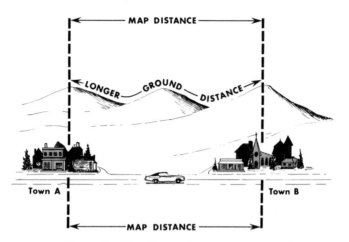

Figure 37. Map distance between towns *A* and *B* on the flat prairie is the same as that between peaks on their respective skylines, yet slope error considerably lengthens the ground distance along the mountainous route.

While slope error is easily illustrated it is not so easily measured in the field. There is no direct method for computing it even with a topographic map, but when accuracy (or whim) demands it, the navigator can get around the problem with a simple computation of *percent of slope* and a reference to the table in *Figure 38*. The percent of slope is the ratio of vertical rise to horizontal map distance, in mathematics referred to as rise over run. Using Perfect Peak once more, its percent of slope would

Figure 38. A table of slope error in measured map distance. Table values are in feet. For example, on a 40% grade (22°) one will walk 385 extra feet per map mile.

98

SLOPE	MAP DISTANCE		
% = X°	1 Mile	½ Mile	¼ Mile
18%/10°	80	40	20
21%/12°	115	58	29
25%/14°	157	79	39
29%/16°	205	103	51
32%/18°	259	130	65
36%/20°	319	160	80
40%/22°	385	193	96
45%/24°	457	229	115
49%/26°	534	267	134
53%/28°	618	309	155
58%/30°	708	354	177
63%/32°	811	406	203
68%/34°	903	452	226
73%/36°	1008	504	252
78%/38°	1119	560	280
84%/40°	1235	618	309
100%/45°	1546	773	387

Figure 38

be equal to 5280 (one mile on the map) divided by 7920. This is .66 or 66⅔%.

The logical extreme of the slope error concept is that a climbing team on a vertical cliff (which has a slope of 90° and a percent slope of 100%) makes no *horizontal* progress at all. Now obviously such a party would be little worried about map distance. *It knows where it is!* Even with the Perfect Peak example, a summit party would have been more concerned with attaining a certain vertical position, but with smaller angles — 20°, 30°, 40° — practical implications come into focus.

Let us first put the significance of slope error into a useful perspective and then go on to the table itself. The table is primarily an *indicator* of how much slope error there may be. (The accuracy with which distances in the field are measured will determine the actual error.) Table values should be interpreted and used according to need. With careful ground measurement table values may be added directly to map distance with good results. This most direct application will come from the need to locate a point position, usually over a reasonably short distance.

For longer trips, especially over rough terrain, the table values will serve as approximations to be considered in general planning. Slope may add two to three miles to a thirty-mile (map distance) backpack in mountainous country. One might stretch a point to make two fifteen-mile days out of thirty, but change his mind on the basis of the probable slope error of up to three more miles with heavy packs.

Whatever the need, slope error will always be in *addition* to map distance. That is, any deviation from the horizontal will lengthen walking distance whether it is up hill or down hill.

When it is decided that (a) an exact point position is of critical importance, or (b) that slope over a long route will add significant distance to the trip, one must compute the percent of slope for the distance as the first step in determining the slope error factor. Here is how:

1. Determine map distance over the entire route.
2. Count the number of contour lines (or spaces) over the entire route.
3. Multiply contour lines times the CI of the map. (This yields the total elevation change over the route. For the error factor it does not matter whether the change is all up, all down, or a combination.
4. With both figures in the same units, usually feet, divide elevation change by map distance.
5. Multiply that decimal fraction by 100 to change it to a percentage.* It is an expression of elevation gain and/or loss over a given horizontal map distance.

Now, to use the table in *Figure 38:*
1. Locate the correct percentage figure in the left-hand column. (In the same box with it will be the equivalent degree of slope.)

---

* Remember, we are discussing slope in relation to horizontal distance, therefore a slope of 45° = 100% because it means a rise of one foot for every one foot of forward progress. Other percent/degree equalities in the table are on the same basis.

2. Follow across the row to the map distance column which best applies. (E.g. for a two-mile route use two times the value in the one-mile column, etc.)
3. Add the total error factor to the measured map distance.

The table range is restricted to practical limits. One will not often encounter slopes over 45° in walking trips. It is usually considered as "climbing" at that angle or above. And below 10° one will rarely be concerned with (or be able to detect) slope error. Values between those shown are easily interpolated if necessary.

Here are two examples of how the table and the concept might be used:

#1 POINT POSITION

(a) map distance = ½ mile
(b) slope = 14°
(c) table value = 79′

½ mile = 2640 feet
+ 79 feet
―――――
2719 feet
corrected
map
distance

#2 A LONG TRIP

A two week loop backpack is planned. Ten days on the trail hopefully will average six to eight miles each. Will the actual ground distance fall within tolerable limits? Using the map and the table of error factors the following schedule is worked out:

Trail Day	Map Distance	Slope	Error Factor
1	9 miles	18%	9 × 80 = 720'
2	7 miles	19%	7 × 98 = 686'
3	5 miles	27%	5 × 181 = 905'
4	8 miles	49%	8 × 534 = 4272'
5	6 miles	45%	6 × 457 = 2742'
6	6 miles	32%	6 × 259 = 1554'
7	5 miles	40%	5 × 385 = 1925'
8	6 miles	21%	6 × 115 = 690'
9	7 miles	18%	7 × 80 = 560'

14,054' =
approximately
2⅔ miles of
slope error

Note that the error factor in day four's plans will amount to nearly ¾ of an additional mile of hiking and carrying over very steep terrain. The party may well want to revise its planned campsite locations or plan a day of rest before trail day five. It is in this sort of revelation that the significance of slope error will be found.

Identification

The identification of significant features, both natural and man-made, is partly a matter of knowing the language of maps. We have already noted one important use of lines in map language. In addition to showing relief, lines are used to portray roads, trails, railroads, power lines, and drainage features.

The map legend or margin will contain a partial set of sample line designs as used on that particular sheet.

Another category of map language is composed of various picture symbols. Again, the map legend will show some (but not all) of the symbols used. A very comprehensive list of topographic map symbols is published by the U.S. Geological Survey. Though these symbols are the ones used on their own product, the list is quite representative of all wilderness travel maps. The Survey people will send the list free of charge upon request. (See address at the end of this chapter.)

A third part of map language is color. The color guide of U.S.G.S. sheets is a fairly standard guide:

• Black is used for man-made features; buildings, names, places, and most roads.

• Blue is used for water and permanent snow and ice.

• Brown is used for all contours except where they define permanent snow and ice.

• Green is used as an over-tint to define woodland cover; solid for forests and typical patterns for scrub and orchards.

• Red is used for important roads and subdivision boundaries.

If part of identification is in knowing the language of maps, the rest is a problem of interpretation. What is the relationship among certain lines, symbols, and colors? This is a more difficult matter to write about because basically it comes down to personal experience. Experience at matching map after map to the land each represents. It will help, however, to present a few facts from the mapmaker's point of view. There is, after all, a limit to what can be said in any language, and map language is no exception. Knowing what the compiler had to consider when putting two and two together should help the map user to come up with the same answer in his interpretation.

If we are to be concerned with what cannot be said, or what must be left out, then the correct word is "inter*p*olation" rather than interpretation. To interpolate means to put between, in effect, to read between the lines.

Reading contour lines is a perfect example of literally reading between the lines. Contour lines represent the shape of the terrain only at specified intervals. The user must be aware that what lies between may be quite different. A contour interval of 100 feet, typical on maps of rugged terrain, leaves a great deal of room for vertical bluffs and deep ravines that might not be shown. Such barriers play havoc with route plans. Further, no contour interval reveals whether a surface is soft grass or a boulder-strewn rubble. The density of underbrush is also left to sad or pleasant surprise.

Relief on nontopographic maps — those without contour lines — may be interpolated with some caution from an adequately shown drainage pattern. Drainage is the collective term for all waterways. The pattern of streams, rivers, and lakes will complement the related ridge and peak structure much the same way that a snapshot complements its negative. A stream denotes a valley whose walls are also the sides of parallel ridges. On the sides of the larger ridges, tributary streams will have carved a sub-ridge system roughly at right angles to the main stream. Note the streams in *Figure 29,* particularly the tributary streams on the southeast side of Scar Ridge.

Where two streams intersect, the point of land between them is likely to be the lower end of a ridge which leads back to a high point. The high points themselves will be located nearer to the beginnings of small tributary streams. Turn to *Figure 29* again and see how Scar Ridge begins at the stream intersection on Miner Flats and rises to the northeast to culminate in High Peak. Most nontopographical maps show a representative pattern of high elevations by "spotting" them, along with elevation figures, over the map.

A great deal more about topography and geology can be deduced from drainage patterns. The interested reader is encouraged to make this an independent study.

In the discussion on map scale it was said that the size of individually shown features (detail) must decrease as scale becomes smaller. Shrinking scale also means that less and less detail can be shown in the same map space. Based upon the purpose of the map, the map scale, and the relative importance of the types of information he has, the compiler must make a choice of what will be shown. When there is a great deal of important material, even some of that must be omitted. Keep in mind that important features will be emphasized and unimportant ones eliminated. Significant features for navigation will rarely be left out.

In the course of depicting detail with a picture symbol some scale distortion will likely occur. In order to be legible the symbols for man-made objects must be given far more map space than their actual size warrants. Some natural features such as small mountain lakes would be nothing more than tiny blue dots if drawn to scale. This is partially compensated for by the fact that as the occurrence of any detail *increases,* its importance as a distinctive landmark *decreases.*

The date that the original survey work was done for a map, as well as the date on which it was compiled or updated, is of prime importance in knowing what to expect of its content. Old surveys are not necessarily any worse or any better than newer ones, but nature and man alike can cause great changes in a few years' time.

One further point to be made in interpreting map detail concerns an interesting technique known as *generalizing.* Because of scale and space limitations, very little map detail can really be shown in full character. A small stream which meanders across a flat meadow is a good example. At a very large scale, perhaps 1/2000, or something used to map plans for a housing project, the stream might be shown in nearly every detail, but at smaller scales, more practical for wilderness travel, such a feature must be straightened or generalized if it is to be shown at all. The same is true for all railroads, drainage, and foot trails.

At 1/62500 a pencil line just one 1/100 of an inch wide represents a strip of land nearly fifty feet wide. A medium duty black-topped road at the same scale becomes more than one hundred feet wide — more like a super highway of eight or nine lanes! Imagine what would happen, then, if all of the curves in a winding ten-foot-wide stream were drawn with a similar pencil line. It would have to become a blur of ink, rather like writing on the head of a pin with a felt tip pen! Instead, the lesser turns are eliminated and the major changes in direction are shown.

Implicit in all of this is a warning: do not take even the best map too literally. Look for significant standout features within a general pattern of detail.

Where To Obtain Maps

There are a great many kinds of maps. So many that we have had to limit our discussion to those suitable for wilderness travel. In the main, these are compiled by the U.S. Geological Survey and the U.S. Forest Service.

Some local sporting goods stores or stationers distribute U.S.G.S. topographic maps, but their selection is often just as local. The two national offices of the Survey have good direct mail-order service for maps covering the entire country. It is best to first write for an index, which will be sent free, and then to order by sheet name and scale from the index. Ask for the index by the name of the state in which you are interested. Enough detail is shown to allow pinpointing of the sheets you will need.

For U.S.G.S. maps *east* of the Mississippi River, write to:

Washington Map Distribution Center
U.S. Geological Survey
1200 Eads Street
Arlington, Virginia 22202

For maps *west* of the Mississippi River, including all of Louisiana and Minnesota, write to:

>Distribution Center
>U.S. Geological Survey
>Federal Center, Building 41
>Denver, Colorado 80225

A second good source of maps is the U.S. Forest Service. These are not topographic maps, but they offer a clear background on which to read all other map detail. The Forest Service is interested in land management, therefore its maps show many access roads and as much other man-made detail as possible in wilderness areas. Maps are available free of charge from specific National Forests, Wilderness Areas, and Ranger Districts. Write to:

>U.S. Dept. of Agriculture
>Forest Service
>Washington, D.C. 20250

Request brochure #FS-13 entitled "Field Offices of the Forest Service." It contains the addresses of ten regional offices from which maps or additional addresses may be obtained. Maps are often in short supply and conservative requests are appreciated.

7 / Pre-Trip Navigation Planning

When memories are counted, any trip that was well planned stands every chance of being recalled as a good one. Planning certainly does not rule out revisions while the trip is in progress. The ability to come through with some good field work – when there has been a change of plans, for example – is one of the joys of wilderness navigating. But careful pre-trip planning, when possible, offers several advantages. First, a thorough map study is the next best thing to first-hand knowledge of an area. Second, weather conditions often make sketching and map reading in the field very difficult or next to impossible. And third, pre-trip planning extends the pleasure of the outing to the comfort of the living room.

110

Every time—and that bears repeating—*every time* you enter a wilderness area, familiar or not, alone or in a group, you should prepare as though you were going in *alone*. In spite of rules, written and unwritten, for following the leader's decisions, or those of the majority, and rules for keeping the party together (as well as rules for *not* going alone) the plain truth is that in the wilderness an individual is potentially a unit of one. This is far from a defense of selfish acts in times of crises. It is an observation which says "be prepared." Leaders have been known to fail, majorities may not materialize, and the best of intentions do not always keep a party together.

The reasons for these failures are more often legitimate than not. Emergencies arise which may leave a party without the full capacities of its trusted leader. Situations which split the party into groups or even individuals are not uncommon. Take, for instance, a party of three, one of whom sustains a serious injury; one must stay with the injured man while the third goes for aid. That third man suddenly becomes a navigator regardless of whether or not he was one on the way in. If emergencies seem remote, it can be promised that anyone who frequents wilderness areas will eventually be involved in some degree of serious problem solving. As a member of a party, each individual owes it to the others to be as fully capable of pulling his own weight as training and experience allow.

Beginner or expert, each member of the party should study the route and form his own pre-trip plan. The beginner who is lucky enough to have a competent leader against whom to check himself is well off indeed. Mistakes will cost the party nothing, and his own price will be small. Just a bit of inner embarrassment!

A pre-trip plan is a map study which results in route plans with compass bearings.

The Map Study

SPECIFIC POINTS TO NOTE

Locate access routes into the area. Auto maps are poor. Forest Service maps are very good, and local inquiries are invaluable. Read your maps carefully for type of roads shown. A small map distance of impassable road may mean an extra day spent backpacking. Do not plan quite so closely, but two such days may cost the party its objective.

Locate starting point and objective on the map.

Plan probable route. Be realistic. Certainly avoid areas for which you are not prepared in terms of equipment, skill, and experience. Unless the party's aim is an untried route, choose the route of least resistance with respect to slope, vegetation, distance, and drainage. Use stream valleys or ridge crests (depending on underbrush), follow powerline rights-of-way, trails, and firebreaks. Ask permission where necessary.

Plan route segments. Put time available against distance and difficulty of terrain. Consider your party's lowpoint in physical conditioning.

Plan campsites. Consider water, fuel, and shelter. Should you carry shelter? Or are man-made shelters available? What of natural protection? Is the country forest covered, partly open alpine meadow, or completely exposed?

General Points

Study general area features.

1. Topographical: Note the shape, steepness, and height of features along the proposed route. Study their spatial relationships to your starting point, to your objective, and to your several lines of travel.

2. Drainage: Note the pattern and frequency of streams. How many swamps, wide rivers, and long lakes must be crossed or detoured?

3. Vegetation: Will your route take you above tree line? At tree line begins a dramatic change in needs involving equipment, skills, and techniques, as well as endurance.

4. Landmarks for navigation: Note fire lookouts, mines, and any kind of road. In short, anything which will fix position or be a source of potential closest aid or escape. Peaks, rock formations, distinctive vegetation, waterways — whatever will be noticed and remembered.

Map Bearings and Route Sketch

A hypothetical route description will best illustrate this phase of pre-trip planning better than a great deal of explanation. Let us suppose that the guidebook or the trip leader has said that the route

. . . ascends the ridge N to within 100 yards of

high cliffs, traverses below cliffs NE to a dry gully, then ascends by way of the gully to the saddle on the summit ridge. From there the summit lies east.

Using the map, while still suffering the comfort of the living room rug, information such as the following should be obtained:

	Distance	Bearings Out	Return
Start to cliffs	2.25 mi.	355°	175°
Cliffs to gully	.75 mi.	55°	235°
Gully to saddle	.2 mi.	38°	218°
Saddle to summit	1.0 mi.	85°	265°
	4.2 mi.		

Remember, as explained in Chapter 6, when taking a True bearing from a map all that is needed is the angle between True North and the objective. It is not necessary to consider magnetic declination.

A better way to record the above information is on a sketch of the proposed route (*Figure 39*). Such a sketch will have to be adjusted or annotated as the trip progresses; readings may change, though not usually a significant amount unless there are gross errors in the map or in the route description. Nevertheless, at all points of change of direction along the way, sketch and bearings should be checked against map and compass. Be certain to observe the over-the-shoulder view as return bearings are carefully noted. A back bearing, remember, is 180° around the compass card from the forward bearing,

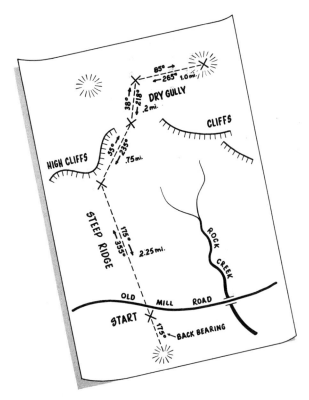

Figure 39. A typical route sketch from pre-trip planning.

115

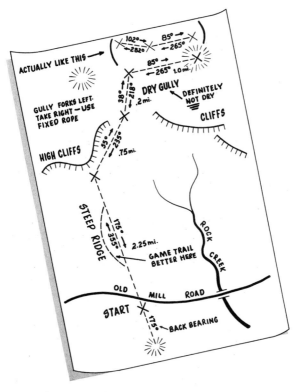

Figure 40. The route sketch from Figure 39 with some notes and revisions once in the wilderness.

or as close to it as allowed by a sighting on a significant landmark. Changes in the sketch will be
in possible route corrections or improvements, and
in the addition of detail concerning landmarks.
Upon reaching the summit the sketch might look
more like the one in *Figure 40*.

In addition to a sketch it is a worthwhile idea to
keep a log of trail and route descriptions. You may
retravel the route in the future, possibly as leader
of your own party. Although the same or even
greater planning would then be called for, some of
the important initial information would be on hand
from which to estimate times, difficulty, etc., for the
group in question. These are typical (for the author)
as-you-go notes:

> Ridge brushy. Fair game trail W side to ½ mile
> before cliffs, then crest better. Time to cliffs:
> 4 hours.
>
> Bad rockfall from cliffs. Descended 200 feet
> for traverse. "Dry" gully wasn't! Gully forks
> after 150 feet. Right fork steep but it goes.
> (We fixed a rope for the return.) Time to
> saddle 2.25 hours. (Spent 1.5 in gully.) Total
> time: 6.25 hrs. Visibility very poor. Sent scouts:
> negative on E lying ridge. Ridge is southeast
> (102°) for short distance, then 85° to summit.
> Time to summit: 7 hours, 15 minutes.

On a bright, clear day the temptation will be
strong to shrug off the pre-trip planning and other
precautions as unnecessary. With the sky a deep
azure blue and the route a virtual straight line,
objective in view, it will seem not remotely possible

that any need for the compass could arise. This is the fatal mistake. The need for the compass does not arise; it *exists*. The need is the need to prevent navigational problems. You only have to retrace a route once during a swirling summer snowstorm or a blinding fog to prove how helpless you are without pre-planning.

8 / *Basic Rules of Wilderness Navigation*

You already have a good start in becoming a competent navigator. You have learned how to operate your own compass. In the process, you have also learned more of the techniques of navigation than you may think. These include:

1. Reading a map.
2. Taking compass bearings from a map.
3. Making a pre-trip map study.
4. Drawing a route sketch.
5. Taking bearings, or using them, in the field.
6. Checking and adjusting bearings at points along the route.
7. Recording notes of route features and times between points.

In the following chapters, you will find additional information on basic principles, techniques, and some of the common problems in wilderness navigation. With these, along with the realization that only experience makes a navigator out of a compass reader, you should be capable of joining any party and assuming your proper share of responsibility.

This chapter will discuss the basic principles of compass navigation, but it should be stressed that these will only be the simplified textbook versions. The real ones are learned in the field where point-lines can take many different forms, and where reference features do not spring up Aladdin-like with a rub of the compass. Though not laws to be rigidly held to, the basics are principles which cannot be ignored. There is nothing selective in them except in how they shall be observed in a given instance.

One of the underlying concepts in navigation is *orientation,* the location of one object relative to another. One of these "objects" is the navigator himself, and the other is any one of the numerous identifiable landmarks of the moment. The navigator's task is to use these landmarks to keep track of how far and in what direction his party has moved.

While orientation pertains to where the party *is,* the idealized pattern of where it *should be,* at various stages of its route, is described by a set of three lines. These, along with orientation, will be found in the four basic tenets of wilderness navigation. They are:

1. Orient all movement to identifiable terrain or man-made features.

2. Travel along planned *point-lines*.
3. Move toward the *line which contains the objective*, then along that line *to* the objective.
4. Plan a *base-line* to back up the return to the starting point.

Orient all movement to identifiable terrain or man-made features.

The navigator must always know where he is in *relation to something else*. (The reverse of that condition is *dis*orientation, which of course means that he is lost.) A series of identifiable landmarks becomes a route with its anchor point, the starting place, associated with safety, food, and shelter. Uppermost in the navigator's mind at all times should be remaining oriented—back through the chain—to the start.

In navigating on land, some sort of reference feature is always possible. (Special techniques are required when the line of sight is severely shortened by weather or voided by featureless terrain, but for this chapter we will assume that visibility is adequate.)

As the party moves toward a final goal, the navigator must be aware of reference features in all directions, not only those along the line of travel. He must frequently turn around to note how the whole landscape will appear on the return trip. This over-the-shoulder view is most important. Rarely does the back side of a terrain feature look very much like its fore side. Common sense might suggest that the party will remember to look back, but this is often not the case. It is truly amazing how easily time and unnoticed miles slip by when the weather is fair and the party is fresh. Even in hard going, perhaps a long arduous climb, a trance-like euphoria overtakes the hiker, while the backward view disappears forever. Many a group has ignored its return route until it has become painfully apparent that finding the way back is not simply a matter of reversing the clues.

The other three basic tenets are concerned with imaginary lines. The first of these, one we already know, is the point-line, or the party's line of travel. The route itself is a series of connecting point-lines. The other two lines are reference lines, ideally locatable at right angles to the line of travel. Their function is to help locate the objective and, on the return trip, to re-locate the starting point (*Figure 41.*)

Travel along planned point-lines.

The point-line is the planned line of travel between the starting point and the objective of each route segment. It represents the longest straight-line sighting distance over which the same two identifiable reference features can be kept in view. In most cases following the point-line will be a matter of observing the rules for taking, using, and field-checking compass readings, always being careful to remain oriented to that "something else." The sequence of steps is illustrated in *Figure 43.*

Move toward the line, which contains the objective, then along that line to the objective.

Tenet number three, for lack of a more imaginative name which captures its essence, is shown in *Figure 41* as the *objective-line.* It forms one upright of the "H." The idea is one we use in getting around in an unfamiliar city. We first choose a highway (point-line) which will intercept the cross street (objective-line) containing the house we want. Then we proceed

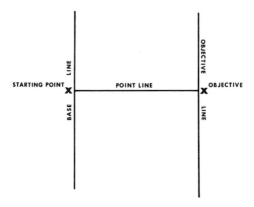

Figure 41. An idealized layout of base-line, point-line, and objective-line at right angles to one another.

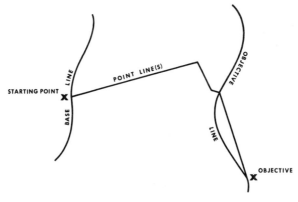

Figure 42. A more probable (or better than usual) layout taken from the pre-trip route sketch in Figure 39.

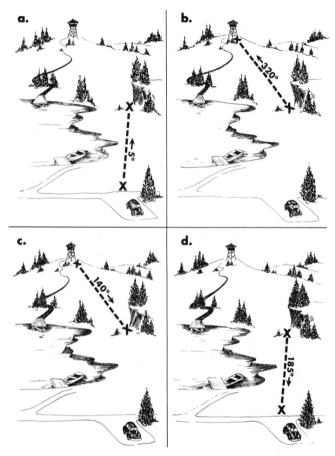

Figure 43. A route of segments, each of which is a point-line from one identifiable feature to another. Steps *c* and *d* are back bearings, exactly 180° the reverse of steps *a* and *b*.

along that line to the specific address. It would not make sense to ignore the major cross street and head across lots for the house number alone.

The problem is similar to a situation in which a navigator must strike out across country toward an objective which will not come into general view until the party is quite close to it. Hopefully the map study will show the objective to lie between two other features which are identifiable and visible from the party's line of travel. These will form the cross street that marks where the party must make its turn. Before reaching that point (in fact, before the party will know that it has reached that point) the navigator will take map bearings on the two features at the point where the line between them crosses his point-line on the map.

We know from Chapter 1 that as the sighting position is moved, bearings taken on the same features will change. As *Figure 44* suggests, this lets the navigator know whether he is approaching the objective-line or traveling away from it. As he approaches it, the angle between the two bearings will become wider and wider with successive sightings. In the perfect arrangement, such as that in *Figure 44,* the angle will widen to a full 180°, which is a straight line.

There will be times when a planned objective-line is unnecessary. When the objective lies *on* a well-defined line of travel, perhaps on a stream course, in a narrow valley or canyon, or on a ridge, there should be little trouble in going directly to it.

The technique of choosing a point-line relative to the objective-line will vary according to the nature of the objective or the type of terrain it is in. The more often the objective comes into view, the more di-

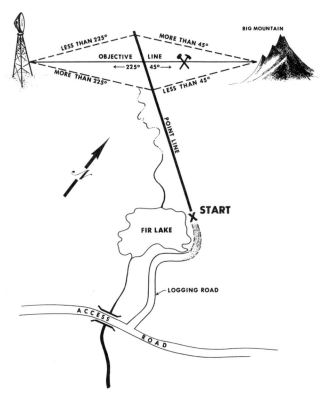

Figure 44. Features not readily identifiable on the landscape may be found by locating the objective line. There is only one place where bearings taken on the tower and mountain will match those obtained from the map showing the mine (crossed miner's picks).

rectly toward it the navigator can move. Contrasting examples of such objectives are a fire lookout and a waterfall. The tower will of course be much easier to locate since it is built to be seen; the point-line can be plotted rather directly to its base. Finding the waterfall will be more difficult. Even if the navigator recognizes the obvious built-in objective-line he may not know which way to turn when he comes across the stream. As with the example of the unfamiliar city, it is wise to plot the point-line a few degrees to one side of the objective itself, to be more certain of which way to turn. This will mean some extra distance to travel, but it will lessen the chance of wandering around in search of a point location. It is exasperating, for example, to reach a lake shore on which you know your camp is located, and not know which way to go to reach it.

Plan a base-line to back up the return to the starting point.

The base-line is the line which backs up the starting point in exactly the same manner that a wire screen backs up home plate on a baseball field. In our case it forms the second upright of the "H" in *Figure 41*. A base-line must be some elongated feature such as a road, river, trail, ridge, firebreak, power line, etc., which forms a backstop to the line of return travel. Like the objective-line, it should be as close to a right angle as possible when it crosses the point-line.

Often the starting point will be on a perfect baseline. We frequently enter wilderness areas from roadside parking lots, trails along rivers, lake shorelines, and the like, however, just as often we enter at the end of a road or at the point where a trail peters out at tree line. Here care must be taken to be aware of a base-line of some sort even if it lies a considerable distance behind the starting point. Once certain it has missed its entry point, it is better for the party to do a little brush thumping out to a base-line than to wander aimlessly in search of the missed point location.

The main road to the east of the lake in *Figure 44* is a good example of a distant base-line. If the party should stray to the left of the point-line on its return to the logging road it would have the main road for a backup. If the miss were on the right of the point-line, the lake itself would be an effective base-line. In this example the lake makes it very plain on which side of the point-line the party has missed its mark, so if it did wander to the left the sensible thing to do would be to make a sharp right, or west, turn and strike the logging road going in to the lake. Without the lake, however, the logging road would be a poor base-line because the party could not be certain which way it had drifted. A wrong turn in search of the logging road could be serious. The main road is farther away, but a far superior base-line.

The closer the base-line to the start the more security it will offer. To a weary group an extra five miles is demoralizing and potentially hazardous. There are always risks in a forced night in the open. It is not irony but fact that the severe weather conditions which deliver the tragic blow when it comes are often the reason the party missed its route in the first place. It follows that a broad base-line may be a life saver as well as a step saver.

9 / *Knowing Where You Are*

Orientation is knowing where you are in relation to something else, and point position is a specific statement of orientation. It says, "Here on the map are all of these reference features, and right here (X) is where . . ."

The exact place "where . . ." can be one of two different positions. It can be the place where you are, or it can be the place where you should be! It may also be plotted in order to record a location to which someone wishes to return — perhaps the site of some cached supplies, a favorite campsite, the best fishing hole.

Whatever the need, plotting point position on the map is relatively simple in clear weather, the exact technique depending upon how much is already known about the party's position. The more is known the easier the plot becomes.

Position knowledge may conveniently be divided into three situations: The party knowing only its *area position* will have the most work to do. *Line position* is one step better. The party knowing its line position will be certain that it is traveling along a particular stream, ridge, road, or some other elongated feature. The third situation is of course *point position,* the certainty of knowing where along a line the party is located. Getting from line position or area position to point position is a matter of taking either one or two bearings and plotting them on the map.

The U.S. Forest Service uses a technique called *intersection* to pinpoint the location of forest fires from its lookout towers. We will be doing very much the same thing, so let us see how it works.

A fire lookout tower is positioned so that as much as possible of its field of view is overlapped by that of other towers. In this way two or more lookouts can watch and report on each general area. In the center of its observation room, each tower has a circular metal table which is imprinted with a full 360° azimuth compass circle. Like a compass card, the azimuth circle has been oriented to True North for use. But rather than having a compass needle, the table is fitted with a sighting device which can be rotated to sight along any bearing from the tower.

When one lookout spots smoke, he quickly takes a bearing on the fire and calls it in to headquarters. By this time a second tower has probably made a similar report and headquarters goes to work (*Figure 45*). On a large map of his district the fire warden locates the two reporting towers and lays out a line along each bearing given to him. The point of *intersection* of the lines is the approximate location of the blaze.

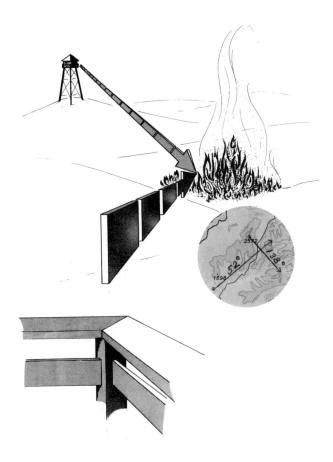

Figure 45. The technique of *intersection* uses cross
bearings from two or more locations to plot
a point position.

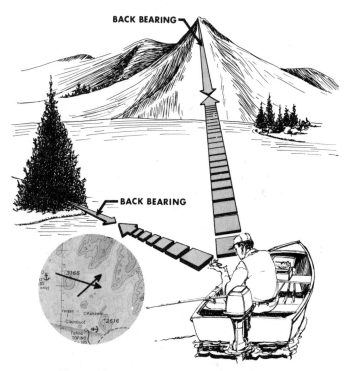

Figure 46. *Resection* is the reverse of the intersection principle of plotting a point position.
It uses crossed *back bearings* to determine the
point position from which the two forward
bearings were taken.

132

The reverse of this technique is appropriately called *resection.* It means that the two bearings will be taken *from the place where they intersect,* namely, the navigator's position (*Figure 46*). To plot where that intersection falls on his map, the navigator will first compute the back bearings, then go through the same steps as the fire warden.

Here is how to plot point position when only *area position* is known:

1. Choose two features about 90° apart. (This will reduce plotting error.) Call them *A* and *B*. Each must be identifiable on the ground as well as on the map.
2. Take True bearings on each feature and compute their back bearings. These will be True bearings from the features to your position, just as though sighted by two fire lookouts.
3. Place the compass or a protractor at *A* and pencil in the back bearing. Do the same at *B*. (One of the free edges of the map, flopped over into position, makes a pretty fair straightedge.)
4. Your *point position* is approximately where the two lines intersect.

If the intersection is obviously *not* your point position (when for example it puts you dead in the center of Lost Lake) then first make certain that the compass sightings are correct. Check your identification of the two features and your computation of the back bearings. Try a third or a fourth bearing to see if they intersect in the same place. If all of these do not change the result (and whatever you were using for a straightedge is worthy of the name) there is only one thing left to do. Check the water depth around you; you may not be *exactly* in the center of the lake.

When *line position* is known only one feature needs to be identified in order to plot *point position*. In the example above the back bearing from either "A" or "B" would intersect the known ridge or stream being followed by the party. Again, in the interest of accuracy, the bearing selected should intersect line position as nearly as possible at a 90° angle.

When visibility is poor the ordinary rules of navigating are not quite adequate. The establishment of point position takes on both a new urgency and a new dimension. The urgency is of course the party's safety, and the new dimension is the measuring of distance traveled (along a known bearing) from the last sure position. By knowing this distance and converting it to map distance, approximate point position may be obtained at any time. The process may be likened to a serious kind of treasure hunt in which the navigator draws his treasure map as he progresses. It will be in terms of so many feet (paces, rope lengths, etc.) on a bearing of X°; so many more on a new bearing of XX°; and so forth.

Maintaining a Straight Line of Travel

Though the idea for maintaining a straight compass line is the same, the technique has to be altered when visibility seriously deteriorates. The basic idea is to keep two distant reference features in view, one oriented to the goal and the other to the previous starting point, and to walk the bearing between them. But the very element of easy navigating which disappears in the mists is of course the identifiable reference feature. As visibility is cut down sighting distances shorten, until, when down to a few feet, sighting distance becomes meaningless in the usual sense for compass work. In spite of it, in order to use the compass with a degree of assurance, the same ideas of the point-line and of taking compass bearings must be made to apply. In a figurative sense, and at times quite literally, the straight line which cannot be sighted must be constructed by the party as it moves.

The most effective and efficient method for laying out such a line along a compass bearing is by using human reference features. The leader designates a teammate to go ahead of the party *to the limit of visibility.* Then, compass in hand, he signals the man left or right to a position on the intended line of travel (*Figure 47*). The party catches up and the process is repeated. By keeping track of the length as well as the direction of each zig and zag in the route, and doing some careful map work, the navigator will have a running assessment of the party's approximate point location.

One hitch in this or any similar method is the reduced length of the segments laid out. The reader will remember that we talked about obtaining the *longest* possible straight-line distance for use as a route segment. The reason is that as the number of sightings increases, so does the chance for error. If a navigator can see from A to Z he can travel it without error (also without a compass). If he must go from A to M (because he cannot see Z) and then to Z, there are *two* chances for error. And if he must make four segments of the route, there will be four corresponding chances for getting off course. Errors will include both sighting and walking the bearings.

Figure 47. Laying out a true course on a feature-less landscape using a human reference point.

136

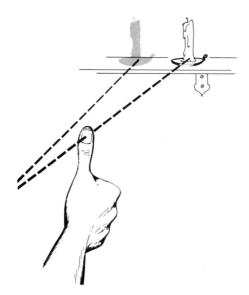

Figure 48. Sighting with the dominant eye will preserve the alignment when both eyes are open. The "weaker" eye will allow a distant object to jump out of alignment.

(*Figure 48* shows how sighting with the dominant eye preserves alignment.) Small errors compound into large ones, and for some unexplained reason, human beings tend to make their errors predominantly on one side or the other, adding them into a circular total. With the compass it is rather difficult to actually circle back on one's starting point, but relatively easy to drift laterally enough to miss the objective.

137

When sighting distances are many and short, as for example when traveling through a wooded area using individual trees as reference features, a partial control on the compounding of error may be exerted by stacking reference features. The navigator moves from 1 to 2 by lining up 1, 2, *and 3*. He then moves from 2 to 3 by lining up 2, 3, *and 4,* etc. With points 2 and 3 used in successive sightings, the effect is to extend the line to the total length of all four features and thus to cut down on errors.

Measuring Distance on Foot

There are several ways to approach distance measure. None of them is satisfactory in all cases and all yield rough approximations at best. As with most systems for doing anything, the price of the easier and faster methods is paid in terms of reduced accuracy. In selecting a method, one should keep these considerations in mind:

- The degree of need for accuracy.
- The time available.
- The amount of help available.
- The equipment on hand to do the job.
- The terrain over which the measure is to be made.

Estimating Distance

When a broad approximation will do, the quickest estimate of distance can be made from the party's elapsed travel time on a particular segment of the route. Someone else's estimate is always third rate, but here is a rough guide to distance and time. Use it as a yardstick in determining your own estimates of what you can do:

Walking Times For One Mile*

	Easy Trail	Difficult Trail
No Pack	20 minutes	40 minutes
Full Pack	40 minutes	60 minutes

* Up and down grades are averaged together.

It is distinctly improbable that any set rates can be given for off-trail navigating and climbing, precisely what this book is most concerned with. The variables of terrain, vegetation, weather, and altitude are just too much to put into a form, no matter how liberally adjusted. To these we can add age, sex, health, and physical condition.

It is clear that some sort of actual measure would be preferable to a "guestimate" of distance by elapsed time. The pedometer is the only mechanical device for measuring walking distance which is at all accurate. It works on the pendulum principle, with the pendulum clicking off a preset amount each time the leg or hip swings forward. Since its only hope for accuracy is the even pace-length of the operator (whose average stride has been predetermined), the pedometer is even less reliable for off-trail navigating than the elapsed time-method. It is fun to use around town and on established trails, but is useless in the wilds where a stride may vary from a leaping lunge through brush to inching ones way up 40° and 50° slopes.

There is a class of optical instruments known as range finders which is surprisingly accurate at measuring crow-flight distance. For wilderness travel, however, they have two serious shortcomings: (1) they depend upon a clear line of sight; and (2) there must be an object of known height at the end of the distance one intends to measure. This latter factor is critical since range finders work on a basis of ratio of optical image size to real size. The optical image size of an object of known height will vary with the distance from the sighting point. For example, a 6-foot man may have an image size of 1 inch at 100 yards, ⅜ inch at 200 yards, and so on at a decreasing rate. The problem in wilderness travel is that frequently there are only rocks, trees, hills, and such in the distance, all of unknown and varying heights. Range finders are excellent for other pursuits, in particular small-boat navigating, hunting, and golf, all of which are usually conducted in the vicinity of objects of known height.

Another system of measuring distance is to count paces. The number of paces times the average length of one pace gives distance. Rarely, however, does the need for measuring distance justify the monotony of counting oneself into a stupor over long distances. (In off-trail terrain the method suffers the same problem of inconsistent pace length that makes the pedometer impractical.) Pace counting has good application in the running of compass courses where distances are shorter, terrain is usually kinder, and monotony is tempered by a spirit of competition. It will be more fully explained in a later section.

A more practical approach is possible with roped parties. These have a more or less known length of line between members that can be used as a unit of measurement. The lead man makes a conspicuous mark in the snow or on the ground. When the end man passes that mark he signals the lead man to make another and the navigator keeps track of the number of "mark" signals he hears, each one standing for a rope length of so many feet. Tallied for each change of direction, and converted to map distance, the party has a fairly reliable indicator of its position in relation to the last known point of safety.

Any of the methods outlined (elapsed time, pacing, or the counting of rope lengths—even the pedometer) will be found suitable at some time or another. A party will not usually measure out a whole route or even a whole mile. The greatest use for distance measure will be in pinpointing critical spots in the route plan. When these occasions arise, the navigator will consider the circumstances—time, help, equipment, terrain, and the degree of need for accuracy—and choose a method. Here is just one hypothetical example:

The party, according to its route description, must move one-half mile northeast from Big Rock (where it presently is located) to ascend a gully on the south side of the summit ridge. A map bearing reveals the gully to lie on 70°. Finding the correct turn is of course critical and accuracy is essential. The party's circumstances upon which the navigator must judge are as follows: Visibility is about fifty yards. The terrain is such that pacing is out of the question. Help, time, and equipment are no problem. (The party has and needs no pedometer, but it is traveling roped for safety.) The leader quite logically decides that the rope-length method will be fastest and most accurate. The best alternative would have been the party's elapsed time, based upon the previous segment of the route.

It is determined that three men traveling on a standard 120-foot climbing rope leave about 100 feet of rope between end men. With one-half mile to go the counting is easy; there are 2,640 feet in a half mile, about 26 or 27 rope lengths. The rest is pure fiction, but a likely result is that the party will come upon a promising gully soon after making its measured turn. And just as likely it will be the wrong one! A little lateral scouting, however, should locate the correct route and a bit of careful navigating will have paid off again.

Although distance measure is rough at best, it will often be the only basis for making an intelligent decision. In any case, it will be more reliable than a guess, and it will surely save time and energy, perhaps even a psychological crisis when impressions in the party differ strongly.

Tying in to the Last Known Point of Safety

If a person ventures into the wilderness very often, especially on terrain which affords little by which to navigate when weather is poor, he will almost certainly have the experience of not knowing exactly where he is or where he is going, even with the most careful of navigating. The point? When a party cannot know for certain where it is going, *it had better be certain of where it has been.* Do what you will with questionable distance measures, but the party must in some way remain oriented to its base camp, the trail head, or some other point which means food and shelter.

With the uncertainties of establishing point position under conditions of poor visibility, it will be far better, rather than to rely on distance measure alone, to maintain a *physical* tie to the last known point of safety. Bear in mind that this point of view assumes a respected bit of route-finding philosophy: that the party's safety comes before the attainment of the objective.

A tie to a safety point can be achieved in the deepest fogs or most barren of terrains by actually marking the route (in some conservation-minded and litter-free way). In forested land or brushy country it is best to use strips of bright-colored cloth or ribbon tied to the vegetation at regular intervals or at least at critical or misleading points. In featureless terrain such as flat plains, sand dunes, or snowfields, lightweight bamboo wands (brightened or not with ribbon) can be left in place along the party's track. The total distance and direction of each small turn will no longer be a major factor in the party's safety; the way back will lie in retracing the route laid out by the markers.

Leaving markers along a route is perhaps an obvious technique, but the spacing of markers is less so and even more critical. In good weather one should be guided by what conditions might become rather than what they are at the outset. Secondly, one should never assume that footprints in snow will be there to follow back. To be of use if the worst materializes, markers must be placed at close enough intervals that a new one may be located before contact with the previous one is lost. A roped party, then, must place its wands about 100 feet apart for maximum safety. When necessary, its lead man can grope about for the next wand while the end man remains oriented to the previous marker. Two or more rope teams traveling together may place wands much farther apart. Two rope teams — disciplined to remain in contact — form two links of a chain that allow spacing to be doubled.

Parties traveling in wooded areas or unroped in other than glacial conditions may judge the spacing of markers by voice contact. On the upper slopes of New Hampshire's Presidential Range, for example, summer conditions of visibility often approach zero, yet these inviting and deceptively low summits draw many inexperienced and unprepared persons each year. To help them find their way over the boulder-strewn ridges, trial crews have constructed large rock cairns at reasonably close intervals. A party can find its way by allowing one of its members to search *well within voice contact* for the next cairn, while every-one else *stays together* at the previous one. The party is guided to each new marker by shouts from the lead man. Cloth or bamboo markers must be placed with the same technique in mind. They will do little good if you become lost between markers.

The need for party discipline in staying together for using a well-laid trail of markers cannot be over-emphasized. How easy it is for stragglers to be left behind! And conversely, how very difficult to hold oneself back when he is stronger than a tired companion and car or camp beckons! Keep in mind, though, that safety may depend on doing so. One man alone may be lost between markers placed for a group, and the anxious first man may wind up going back to look for his fellow.

10 / Staying On Course

The pat lists of steps so readily presented in the first half of this book for performing one or another compass function have appeared far less frequently in this part. The difference is between theory and practice.

Once out of the classroom and into the woods one quickly learns that a wilderness is not crisscrossed with strings of reference features waiting like highways to take the navigator any place he wishes to go. And none of us would have it any other way. To remove the challenge is to remove the joy of being in the wilds. Though there are no "five easy steps" to making the transition from book to field, a rundown of the problems — and some of the solutions — does help.

Our major concern in this chapter is in staying on course once it has been selected. The best way by far to discover the difficulties involved is to put the book down, pick up the compass, and take a compass walk, in particular a "beeline" compass walk. The "beeline" is a sighted straight line between two points, and the beeline walk, as its name implies, is a straight-away-turn-for-(almost)-nothin' course from one point to another. After reading the ground rules, try one for yourself. In addition to having a built-in object lesson this exercise is a lot of challenging fun.

The object is to choose two points which cannot be kept in view while traveling between them. This can be done by sighting the end point from a hilltop starting point, or, using a map, by selecting an objective which cannot be seen from the starting point. Using the compass only, the hiker is to navigate from track to tree or barn to bush in as straight a line as possible to the end point.

Choose a short distance for the first try. A half mile or so will make the point nearly as well as a mile. The walk will also be more instructive if an area of relatively unfamiliar ground is selected. The hillier the country, the better will be the lesson.

Some detours will obviously have to be made. Trees and buildings on your track are to be skirted. Depending on your own determination, physical fitness, and degree of technical skill, such detours as those for streams, lakes, and rock barriers are optional, but all else is climbed, pushed aside, or jumped until the objective is reached. Try it.

The difficulty encountered in holding to the selected course under conditions where the objective cannot be seen, especially when such drastic beeline attempts are made, will bring out some of the limitations of the compass in wilderness navigation. The person who tromps off into the wilds had better know what these are in order not to expect more from the instrument than it can deliver.

In theory, a particular compass reading or bearing is a unique bit of fact. That is to say, there is one and only one True bearing between any two points on earth. In practice, however, the magnetic compass is not nearly sensitive enough to support the theory. Even the most sophisticated of surveying instruments, which, like the compass, also measure angles, usually obtain slightly different readings on successive sightings, and these are optical instruments not subject to the whims of the earth's magnetic field. With the unsophisticated magnetic compass the amount of error can reach noticeable proportions. Let us list this and other points to be aware of:

1. Most compasses cannot be read to an accuracy of more than plus or minus 1°. Manufacturers leave it to the user to estimate between tickmarks of 5° or even 10°, yet an error of only 1° at a distance of one mile means about ninety-two feet of lateral error.

2. Magnetic declination is not stable (*see* Chapters 1 and 5).

3. Declination taken from a map or from a chart is an average for an area. Small, and *usually* unimportant, local differences exist.

4. All maps have some error in them. Even the very best, the U.S.G.S. topographic quadrangle sheets, claim no better than a consistent positional accuracy of 100 feet, yet a pencil line of

.02 inch in width represents from forty to a hundred feet of ground distance depending on scale.

Put another way, these factors mean that a navigator will not always be able to obtain the accuracy desired—through no fault of his own. Coupled with this is a seemingly strange human inability to walk a straight line given the correct one to do it on! Apparently, then, since sightings within a 3° or 4° band are hit or miss (and walking a straight course has no better chance), holding to a given compass bearing may not be taken for granted to say the least.

The subject of compass inaccuracy is best left with a warning to be aware of its probable influence. The methods for holding to a course are based on its occurrence. In many cases greater accuracy itself is not critical, and further, such errors mostly tend to cancel one another out.

Using Reference Features

The compass provides only the forward component of navigation. By itself it has no way of preventing lateral errors. This as we know is where the use of reference features fits in. Using the compass without consulting reference features for control of lateral drift is known as *compass following* (*Figure 49*). Very much like drawing a twelve-inch line with a one-inch ruler—in one stroke.

Here is a hypothetical example of compass following. Suppose that the first leg of a route is from a hilltop to a footbridge crossing a stream in the valley below (*Figure 50*). The navigator takes his initial sighting, records it, and starts down the hill. Let's

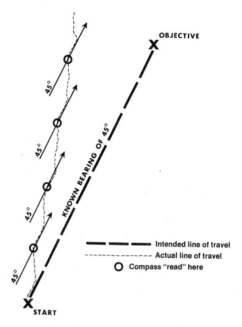

Figure 49. Using the compass without consulting a distant reference feature is known as compass following. It results in the kind of lateral error shown here.

say his bearing is 187°. At some point he will lose the direct view of his objective. When he feels the need for a check on his heading he will take out his compass, orient it to True North, and again set out *in the direction* indicated (but *not* toward a specific objective). The process may be repeated any number of times, but soon the navigator will have no means of determining whether or not he has drifted laterally from his intended line of travel. At no time will the compass give a hint of the slowly accruing error;

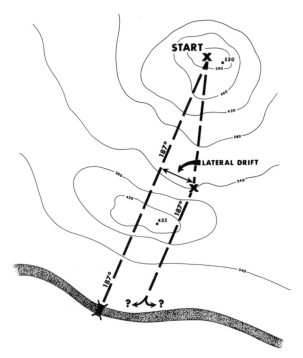

Figure 50. A case of compass following. The navigator apparently discovered his errant ways at X, but a substantial lateral error has already occurred and may cause him grief in locating the footbridge.

however, each time consulted it will dutifully confirm that a course of 187° does indeed exist at that spot.

Reference features, the alternative to compass following, appear to be the obvious key to controlling lateral drift. The compass yields a direction, the navigator chooses a feature coinciding with the bearing, *and then the compass is put away.* In areas of heavy vegetation, however, or in wide-open country lacking in distinctive features, it may be more difficult than obvious in practice. Most of the nonmountainous parts of our country are in this category and for them more positive techniques are needed.

The point-line does have some special usefulness in spite of scarce reference features and the imprecisions of the magnetic compass. It is in theory the best possible line of travel, though the actual line will be the easier zigzag course to both sides. The original bearing can act as a standard to which movement is referred. The navigator in the footbridge example might have anticipated losing direct sightings on his objective and so have noted some other feature on the horizon behind it. With drift to his left, compass checks on the skyline backup feature would show readings of *more* than 187°. To correct for drift he would know to move to the right, decreasing the bearing value of his occasional sightings until back on course at 187°.

If no skyline checkpoint is available behind the objective, it may be possible to use the starting point in similar fashion. In the case at hand the navigator would have had to move to his right until a sighting taken on some feature associated with the starting point gave him a bearing of 7° (the back bearing of 187°).

Bracketing

When no outstanding features present themselves forward or backward on the point-line, points not on the point-line must be used. Remember, *all movement must be referred to something.* Such use of off point-line features, and there are several variations, may be called *bracketing* the objective. The task is simply to plot a course in relation to the chosen features rather than directly toward them. The landmarks will define limits. Thinking will be in terms of "*between* the tower and the tall pine," or "*to the south* of High Point on the north bank of the river" rather than "*from* Old Baldy *to* the wet cliffs."

In practice, casual bracketing is used as often as point-to-point navigating. If one's objective is a spring at the base of a hill, it hardly makes sense to climb the hill simply because it is the identifiable landmark. The knowledge that the party is passing by or between its check-points is just as informative as is touching them, and is infinitely more satisfying in terms of progress toward an objective.

More definite bracketing may be employed to locate the starting point on the return as well as to find the objective on the way in. The technique is identical to planning an *objective-line* as discussed in Chapter 8. The navigator steers between two prominent features which form a line across the party's line of progress (as nearly at right angles as possible). When map bearings are matched by field bearings, the party is either at its objective or on a line containing one or both reference features and the objective as well. When the technique is used to bracket the starting point for the return trip, it is better to choose the bracketing features before the party sets out, obviating the need (and error potential) for map bearings.

Unavoidable lateral drift may cause problems where bracketing with terrain or man-made features is not clear-cut or even not possible. If any difficulty is anticipated, the party may place its own "features" along the base-line before starting out. Each bracket is a numbered or color-coded marker set out in sequence so that it reveals the direction of the starting point along the base-line. All markers will of course identify the base-line itself, so each serves two purposes. Properly coded and spaced, markers will in addition yield the distance to the start.

Frequently, because the base-line is a road or a trail, a river or a lake shoreline, it is a simple matter to place enough markers for good route assurance. The greater the distance from the final objective back to the unsure starting point, the more markers should be placed. Here is an example of bracketing in practice:

A party's objective is a distinctive bluff some three miles from an old logging road. There is no problem on the way in because the bluff rises high enough to be seen frequently, but looking back along the return route the party will be confronted by a sea of undifferentiated forest. The old and fading road can hardly be seen. Once back into the trees and on gently rolling ground, the usual techniques with reference features will be largely out of the question.

Hitting the logging road base-line should pose no problem; the party will have its original bearing on the bluff. The computed back bearing, along with occasional sightings on the bluff, should keep the party on at least an adequate course. We may suppose that the group eventually does come upon its base-line. But *where* along the base-line? Are the cars to the left or the right?

Knowing beforehand what the problems will be,

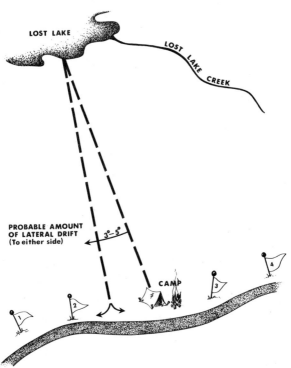

Figure 51. With no prominent natural reference features to line up on, a party may use pre-placed bracketing markers along its baseline to indicate the direction it must turn to reach an inconspicuous objective.

the party has placed bracketing flags along its base-line running from #1 at the north end to #4 at the south end (*Figure 51*). (Different colors north and south would have worked fine.) The starting point lies halfway, between flags #2 and #3. With such a well-defined base-line the spacing interval decided upon is about 200 yards.

Let us say that on his arrival at the old logging road the leader judges that the party is south of its mark. Accordingly, they turn north, promptly come across flag #4, which will tell the party that: (a) it is on the correct logging road; (b) that it must turn (or continue) to the north; and (c) that the distance to the cars is only about 300 yards.

Many a wilderness traveler has come out of the woods on what he believes to be the correct road only to find out some weary hours later that he was wrong. Others have come out upon the correct base-line, changed their minds, and plunged back into the wilds to spend a cold night in the open. The placing of bracketing markers is good insurance for anyone entering the wilderness, but is especially so for rockhounds, geologists, hunters, mushroom collectors, etc., who usually do not follow definite courses. Not only do these pursuits encourage wandering, but they practically prohibit paying close attention to the route itself.

The best method of accounting for uncontrollable lateral drift is to anticipate it and build it into the route plan. This is a particularly good idea in areas of indistinctive terrain. The preceding bluff-logging road route example is a case in point. (This, incidentally, is the method taught to soldiers who must often travel in strange surroundings at night and in the thickest possible cover.) Wherever reference features are not visible or else are effectively lacking, the navigator can add a few degrees to the correct compass bearing before starting. For instance, 3° is a reasonable amount of error to expect, so the party can steer 5° to one side of its objective, say the south side of an easterly course. If the drift does not materialize, the party will be off by 5°; if it occurs on the right of its point-line, the error will be as much as 8°; but if it shows itself on the left, between the objective and the point-line, the party will come as close as 2° to the actual bearing of the objective. The point is that wherever the error shows up, the party will know which direction it must take.

Building known error into a route will cause some extra walking, but it will save far more in the long run.

Sources of Navigating Error

There are perhaps as many sources of navigating error as there are navigators to invent them, but here are a few of the more common ones:

- Using poor or outdated maps.
- Failure to observe the four basic tenets of navigation (discussed in Chapter 8).
- Association with point objectives rather than broad lines and features.
- Outdated declination information.
- Mistrusting the compass and relying on "sense" of direction.
- Confusing the north- and south-indicating ends of the needle.
- Out of date or poorly interpreted route information.
- Assuming that declination does not matter.
- Arithmetic errors in conversions from mag to true, etc.
- Entirely avoidable sources of magnetic deviation, such as metals on the person, cameras and light meters, and so forth.

- Failure to account for or control lateral drift.
- Failure to observe the over-the-shoulder view for the return.
- Not using map and compass until already lost.
- Sighting with the wrong eye.

In nearly all persons, one eye is dominant over the other. A sighting taken with the weaker eye may be 5° to 10° off. If you do not know which of your eyes is the dominant one try this simple test: with *both* eyes open, line up your extended thumb with any distant object. Close one eye. Is the alignment preserved? Try the other eye (without moving). One of your eyes will preserve the alignment made while both were open, proving that it is stronger than the other. With only the weaker eye open, the thumb will appear to jump to one side.

11 / Using Nature's Signs

Judging by the booming outdoor business of recent years, there is a vestige of man-the-pathfinder in each of us. It must be because of this Daniel Boonish trait that we are flocking to the wilds in increasing numbers. Or perhaps it is because the little taste that we get puts us so much in awe of the real pathfinders in our history. Either way, we recognize a developed talent in the early woodsman which few today can equal. We marvel at the ability of the Meeks, the Colters, and the Sublettes to navigate thousands of square miles of territory without ever becoming seriously disoriented.

Osborne Russell, another of the sturdy mountain men, has left us a priceless record of just such wilderness route-finding in his *Journal of a Trapper.** His adventures took place in the Rocky Mountains in the colorful fur trapping days of the 1830s and 1840s. Recounting years of seeming wandering, Russell soon leaves the reader thoroughly disoriented and scurrying for the book's maps; while having none himself, he and his fellow trappers seem always to know exactly where they are. Only once does he need admit to being confused, and even then due to an error in judgment.

There is of course a great deal of difference between the mountain man's situation and the latter day adventurer's two-week trek into the same region. A man can hardly be lost if he is self-sufficient and has no particular place to be.

The orientation skills exhibited by men of Russell's breed were learned by constant need and application. The pioneer explored his world step by step with trial-and-error luck, and laid the basis for what we know of the process today. He pieced his experiences together over many trips to form the knowledge which took him from one headwaters to another, crossing high divides, never doubting where he was going or how to return. He gradually put together a big picture of the region, his map where otherwise none existed.

This is exactly what we must do, get the big picture, if we are to emulate him at all. But we must take short cuts because we have less time. Above all we must take greater caution because we have more need.

---

* A Bison book. University of Nebraska Press, Lincoln, Nebraska 1969. Edited by Aubrey L. Haines.

Getting the Big Picture

Few of us will ever be privileged to open up virgin country, but the recompense for having to be second (or more likely ten thousandth) is a storehouse of information with which to start the orientation machinery.

The library is an excellent place to begin any trip. All manner of travel books and regional guides have been written for nearly any place one wants to go. These are the source of hundreds of facts, large and small, about the wider area of interest.

While browsing, be concerned with the local geography — physical and human. The degree and pattern of inhabitation may very directly affect your plans. Certainly the topography and land use will. Find out about natural resources and the type of vegetation cover. Is there mining in the vicinity? Or logging? Besides being interesting in their own rights, mining and logging operations frequently offer access roads. Pay particular attention to climate and rainfall. What conditions can one expect during a June trip — or would September be a better time? It can snow above 10,000 feet in the Rockies anytime of year, and in New England the same is true above 5,000 feet!

There is no better source of information than the person who has gained it the hard way. Unless you live in a small town it is usually possible to find one or more persons who have been where you plan to go. Such individuals are normally more than happy to share their knowledge. Comments such as these help tremendously: "It isn't marked on the map, but there is a good shelter cabin down over the pass about a quarter of a mile. It's on a spur trail just beyond a group of white boulders." Or perhaps, "Be careful

Figure 52. Orientation in the wilderness begins at
home or in the library with a thorough study
of the area of interest.

when you make the portage from Henry Lake to the
Cloud River. You cross a branch of it, but there are
bad rapids farther down. Keep going over the ridge
to the main stream."

Auto road maps, hardly worthy for most considerations in wilderness route-finding, are not only good
sources for the big picture, but are available in most
mechanized countries. A road map will cover a relatively large area around the immediate area of interest and form the larger framework for orientation.
They are better than map atlases because of their
larger scale, and far easier to store and handle in the
car. Study the layout of towns and cities and the major
network of highways. Most such maps will reveal the
trend of mountain ranges, large lakes, and important
rivers.

Do not underestimate the value of this overall view. If one knows that the north-south trending range he intends to hunt is flanked by an Interstate highway on the east and a twenty-mile strip of sparsely inhabited foothills on the west, it seems that he will have to try hard to become very disoriented. At the same time, be careful about accepting very much specific detail from road maps. Most are made by oil companies who naturally emphasize roads with gasoline stations and not the small details of back road systems. Road maps are consequently highly inaccurate in terms of placement of detail and matters of scale. A five-mile misplacement of a certain turn-off means little to the driver of a modern auto, but woe to the tired tramper who depends on its being there.

Closer to the objective area, one needs a clear knowledge of the system of access roads and trails in addition to the ones he *intends* to use. These are his alternate base-lines and escape routes. U.S. Forest Service maps, where available, are excellent for the purpose. (*See* "Where to Obtain Maps," the last section in Chapter 6.) Because of the use the Forest Service makes of them, their maps usually contain late date information on fire roads, logging and other access roads, and trails.

Nature moves fast in obliterating man's scars, and trails are the first to suffer while often being the last to receive repair. It is well before hitting the trail to spend an hour or two in talking with local rangers, fire wardens, area residents, and others for up-to-date reports on trail conditions. The local sport shop is always a good place to visit. Washouts, relocations, new trails, poor maintenance, etc., can make a difference in an otherwise well-planned outing.

Check with these same people on off-trail conditions. The party which takes time to learn snow depths in the canyons, recently logged-off areas, and the presence or absence of good water can save itself much time and discomfort. The leader should also ask permission to use private land, or, if on public property, inquire about camping and campfire regulations.

Into the Wilderness

So here it is — the end of the trail at the end of the road — and the beginning of a startlingly real wilderness. Now the navigator finds that his craft is more than vigilant attention to map and compass. Something of the mountain man's ability is needed to turn a backyard navigator into a confident route-finder.

Part of the secret of the transformation is in becoming a good observer. Thousands of cues must become associated with each segment of the route. Have you ever noticed that a passenger in an automobile rarely remembers the route as well as the driver? The driver is paying close attention at every turn, while the passenger is along for the ride and free to enjoy the scenery. Whoever is at the wheel consequently has fewer gaps in his mental route map because of a greater number of associations, both conscious and subconscious. Though orientation cues in the wilderness are far less distinctive than those on a highway, the process is the same. The difference is that in the wilderness no one can afford to "be along for the ride."

Orientation is a sort of game played in between compass checks with the environment. It consists of actively making the most associations possible.

". . . That bluff due north of the cars is now northwest of us . . . the sun is slightly on our backs and to the right; with the time 10:30, it must be just east of south . . . the creek in the valley to the west is swinging around more easterly to where we will probably cross it . . . be careful going back down the ridge; it forked near the bottom and we came onto the main ridge from the west spur . . ." and on it goes. The idea is not to *get* your bearings periodically, but to *never lose them*.

The ability to properly orient yourself in the wilds is a learned trait. More than that, it is learned in a specific environment. You cannot learn your way around a dark room by walking the backyard blindfolded. The hot-shot mountaineer is easily turned around on the open plains, and the plainsman is as easily befuddled in the mountains. Forests present different situations from those of open lands; sand dunes look nothing like the bottomlands of the Midwest and South; and city streets, where most of us learn our orientation, have nothing in common with any other type of wilderness on earth. Once away from a familiar pattern, the way is easily lost. Anyone making the transition from one setting to the wilderness of a different geographic region must learn a new set of orienting clues.

Orientation Aids

Let us assume that all of the advance orientation has been done. The library work is complete, the road maps and wilderness maps have been studied, and every member of the party has a good overall impression of the lay of the land.

Orientation is knowing where you are in relation to some meaningful point; the road, a town, the parked cars, etc. The route-finder must develop a feeling for distance as well as for direction. As pointed out in Chapter 9, position is a combination of both.

Distance in the wilds is primarily a function of time or pace, but many other things enter in. These might be the age and sex of the party members, weather, terrain, slope, health, physical condition, weight of the pack, and perhaps many more. Ordinarily one need not be preoccupied with time in the woods. Indeed, something is to be said for going there to forget it, but it is well to develop a habit of noting times for distances traveled. Gradually a framework for the distance feeling will be formed and become surprisingly accurate.

Developing direction sense is another matter. Here is where continual observation pays off, that is, as mentioned above by never losing track of where known points are in relation to the movement of the party.

Using the Sun

The sun, provided it is shining, is by far the best direction pointer available to the wilderness navigator. Every schoolboy knows that it rises in the east and sets in the west, but the half-serious navigator can improve greatly on that rule of thumb.

The sun's position in the sky from rise to set is complicated by several factors, but for our purpose we need consider only one of them. The earth does not rotate on a perfectly vertical axis. Instead it actually inclines by $23\frac{1}{2}°$, much like a giant top leaning to one side as it spins. Though the tilt never changes, except for some minor wobbles that take a few thousand years to notice, the position of the tilt relative to the sun changes regularly on a yearly basis.

On June 21 or 22 each year (*Figure 53*), the longest day of the year in the Northern Hemisphere, the upper half of the earth is tilted most directly toward the sun, enough so in fact that the sun shines over the

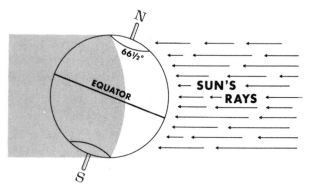

Figure 53. The distribution of daylight over the earth's surface on June 21 or 22, the longest day of the year in the Northern Hemisphere.

top and down the back side to the line of $66\frac{1}{2}°$ N. latitude ($66\frac{1}{2}°$ plus $23\frac{1}{2}°$ conveniently total $90°$, the full latitudinal distance from equator to north pole). This line, traced around the earth, is known as the Arctic Circle. Above the circle there will be no sunset at all this date. As one approaches the pole there will have been none for days or even weeks before that time.

What we are concerned with is the direction of the sun throughout the day rather than with hours of daylight itself, though the two are directly related. In order to shine longer it must stay in the sky longer, and the only way this can happen is for it to make a longer and lower arc. This in turn necessitates rising and setting closer and closer to the north as latitude increases.

On a recent climbing expedition to the coastal mountains of the Skagway, Alaska area, which is about 60° N. latitude, the author's "sense" of direction was constantly confused by the latitudinal extremes of the rising and setting sun. The experience bears out an earlier remark concerning directional cues which are learned in one setting and applied in another.

To the observer standing just below the Arctic Circle, the sun will rise almost due north, but swing all the way southward around the sky before coming back to the north. Here it will briefly set before rising again a few degrees away. All during the day it will have remained just above the horizon, and not far enough below it at "night" to more than dim the light. On a line near the equator the same day the sun will rise and set due east and west. Its climb in the sky will be vertical, being directly overhead at noon. Day and night will be of equal duration. At all other latitudes the sun's position at rise and set as well as during the day will vary within the above wide extremes.

Figure 54 illustrates the approximate arcs in the sky the sun will describe for several sample latitudes. Again we are using one date only rather than complicate the examples with seasonal changes. Note that on the equator the most extreme variation for the year is never more than the $23\frac{1}{2}°$ tilt of the earth, while

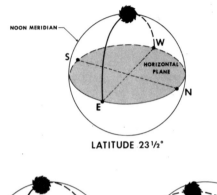

LATITUDE 23½°

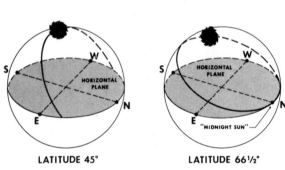

LATITUDE 45°   LATITUDE 66½°

Figure 54. The approximate path of the sun in the
sky on June 21 or 22 at three latitudes. Note that
at 23 ½° the sun is directly overhead, at noon,
while at the Arctic Circle it stays much lower in
the sky all day and merely scrapes the horizon in
the north at midnight.

at more northerly latitudes the effect is increased by
the curving away of the earth.

As the time of year progresses toward December 22
and the shortest day of the year in the northern
hemisphere, the whole picture reverses itself and the
sun will appear to rise and set just as far south as it did
toward the north.

The average sportsman will be doing his route-finding in the mid-latitudes — say from 30° to 60°, though many will go into northern Canada and Alaska. At 30° N. latitude, the southern areas of the United States, the seasonal variations of sunrise and sunset will not be great. At 60°, however, the difference in bearing of the summer and winter sunrises may be as much as 160°; from extreme northeast to extreme southeast. A far cry from the oversimplified "the sun rises in the east and sets in the west!" For the air or sea navigator who moves great distances in relatively short times, extensive tables are available from which to compute the bearings we are talking about. None are necessary for the more stationary wilderness navigator, but he should cultivate the habit of noting the direction of the sun throughout the day. It will quickly become part of the directional sense often wrongly attributed to instinct.

Drainage Pattern

Another very helpful aid to orientation is knowledge of an area's drainage pattern. Rivers and their tributaries can be used much as city arterials and their side streets. Just as with city streets, knowing that a watercourse is going where you wish to go is more important than knowing its compass direction. Following along a trunk stream, the navigator may peg his position at each tributary crossing somewhat like counting city blocks. He will have to take care that he does not mistake a small stream for one which does not actually appear on the map. Remember, in areas of high concentration of detail, especially at smaller scales, the map compiler will be forced to show a representative pattern only.

The drainage pattern provides yet another clue to direction. Rivers naturally conform to the topography of the land they drain. Typically we find two or three major patterns of ridge and river combinations along with some interesting variations to look for. During your sessions with the various maps it will be useful to form an impression of the overall drainage pattern of the area being traversed. This can be especially helpful if you become disoriented, but also, a knowledge of the layout of streams in an area might well be the decisive factor in preventing the "lost" syndrome from developing.

Some typical drainage patterns are shown in *Figure 55*. By far the most common of all is the *branching* pattern. It suggests the root or limb structure of a tree. In this form, as one might expect, the tributary streams join the parent stream with a V angle opening in an upstream direction. The *trellis* pattern features tributaries joining main streams *at right angles*. The parallel valleys and ridges in this type of topography result in longer and narrower drainage basins than in the branching pattern.

Within a branching drainage area one may cross many ridges and feel that he is oriented to the parent stream much as the blade of a fan is oriented to its handle. While all trellis drains also converge to one parent stream eventually, their relationship is more like that of the blade of an oar to its shaft. If one is to follow water out of a trellis drainage area, he had better be prepared for a long walk. On such terrain as this it might be easier to think in terms of orientation to the correct valley or ridge rather than to a single parent stream many miles away.

Geologic processes too complex to go into here are responsible for the various drainage patterns and for

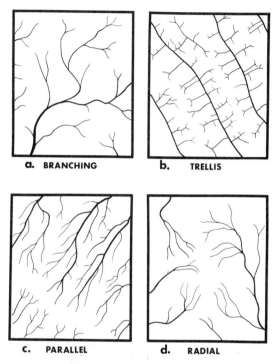

a. BRANCHING

b. TRELLIS

c. PARALLEL

d. RADIAL

Figure 55. Four distinctive drainage patterns. See the text for a discussion of their significance in maintaining orientation.

the more interesting variations. A couple of the variations themselves, however, are important enough to point out. One is the *radial* pattern. It forms on conical or dome-shaped rises. The critical consideration for remaining oriented in areas of radial drainage concerns descending the rise into the correct headwaters. The wrong one will result in drastic error. The volcanic cones of the Pacific Northwest (such as Mounts Hood, Baker, and Rainier) are noteworthy examples of radial drainage, but lesser ones do occur. *Parallel*

171

drainage is similar to the branching pattern but is characterized by closely packed valleys and ridges — as if the fan were partially folded — and by stream junctions which suggest end runs around abruptly sheared ridges. As with the trellis pattern, walking distance in following parallel streams out is a key problem, though not usually as severe.

With some caution one may deduce general geographic direction from any drainage pattern in which streams of the same order parallel each other. If main streams tend to flow *northeast,* first tributaries may flow *northwest,* and so on. Drainage patterns overlap more often than not, sometimes with traces of several forms in a small area. More important than being able to name a particular pattern is being aware of the orientation potential of the one of immediate concern. The implications of any pattern for remaining oriented are often rather subtle, but like learning to read tracks and other signs of the prey, the results of careful study are well worth the effort.

Natural Direction Finders

Along with a caution on relying too much on stream pattern for direction goes a general warning on the sole use of any natural direction finder. Route-finding by natural signs is a skill which requires a great deal of knowledge about a specific area. It is especially true in this context that a little knowledge is a dangerous thing.

The subject of natural direction finders also abounds with half-truths and misconceptions. For example, the one who started the story about moss and the north sides of trees is hopefully spending eternity trying to get out of Pearly Gates National Forest armed with only that bit of knowledge. It is for certain that he never visited western Oregon, Washington, northwestern California, or any other place with more than a moderate amount of rainfall and limited sunshine. The half-truth of it is that moss *can* predominate on the north sides of trees, or, due to light and shade conditions, on any side of a given stand of trees.

When attempting to tell direction by any natural means, it is far safer to trust observations based on large areas, or better, on comparisons of large areas. For example, north slopes will likely be more heavily vegetated than south slopes, but the same may be true of west and east sides of ridges where the west (and windward) side receives heavy rainfall. In any case, look at both sides of several ridges, then check directions with the compass. While in that general area the observation is likely to hold true.

The most interesting and by far the most trouble-making of the misconceptions about natural direction finding is that human beings have an innate sense of direction. Human sense of direction, if anything, is a sense of wrong direction. On a cloudy day, with no prominent reference features to follow, the most practiced woodsman will likely walk a curved path unless he uses a compass.

One idea of why this occurs is that a person turns his head away from wind, sun, or rain, etc., and tends to walk in that direction. This is not a steady turning which might be noticeable, but an accrual of small adjustments which favor one side. Another explanation credits humans with an animal instinct for purposely traveling in wide circles calculated to bring the subject back to his starting point. This idea probably comes from the flight of a rabbit from a predator enemy; if caught on the wrong side of its burrow, a bunny will lead its pursuer on a long circular jaunt in order to reverse the situation. After a chase of a mile or so it simply drops out of sight when it reaches home.

The trait may stand rabbits in good stead, but ungrateful man is not proud of his ability to run around in circles. Perhaps a more plausible answer to the question is only the ability to walk is innate — whether in curved or straight lines — and that man needs to refer his movement to recognizable stationary objects, or, as with the sun, to the known course of a movable object.

Maintaining orientation by natural direction finders requires a high degree of skill. There are wilderness-wise individuals who are that much at home in one or more geographic regions and do use such pointers as the direction of the heaviest branch growth, the turning toward the light of plants, the direction of prevailing winds, and hundreds more. The Suggested Reading List contains a fascinating book on the subject by an obvious expert in his field, but until the wilderness navigator feels quite certain of himself he had better cast his lot with Osborne Russell who had this to say about one of his own moments of disorientation. Incidentally, the spelling and punctuation are Mr. Russell's:

> We were now in sight of the red Butes on the river Platte — which appeared about 40 miles distant SE The next morning we found the weather foggy with sleet and snow falling I tried to persuade my comrades to stop until it should clear away urging the probability of our steering a wrong course as we could not see more

than 200 paces but they concluded we could travel by
the wind and after making several objections to travelling by Such an uncertain guide to no purpose I gave
up the argument and we started and travelled about
ESE for three hours as we supposed then stopped a
short time and built a fire of Sage while it still continued
to snow and rain alternately. and seeing no signs of the
weather clearing we started again and went on till
near Night when the Sun coming out we found that
instead of travelling ESE our course had been NNE
and we were as far from the Platte as we were in the
Morning. . .

Whatever your competence in maintaining general
orientation, retain the habit of making periodic compass checks and keeping the route sketch up to date.
The day will come when you will be glad for the
practice.

12 / Route-Finding Problems

The gauntlet cast at man's feet by the wilderness is an impersonal one, yet in picking it up man accepts the same challenge and adversity as though there were a clash of wills. Finding the way over rough or unfamiliar country inevitably leads to situations not fully anticipated in the most experienced party's planning. Forests and mountains were simply not designed to submit to formulas.

It has been pointed out that the pure science of navigation is concerned with traversing large expanses of air or water along essentially straight lines. Land travel differs in that one usually remains in touch with some physical line, a road or perhaps a trail or river, connecting two points. On such marked routes the technical navigating has already been done.

Wilderness travel takes on the aspects of a science when it is conducted off the beaten track. Unlike air and water navigation, though, straight-line travel in the wilds is rarely possible. Where the physical line is lost, and where the medium — which is solid earth rather than fluid air or water — prevents following the straight path, an entirely new dimension is added. With the addition of solid obstructions, dangerous or difficult alternatives, and a choice at every turn, navigation becomes route-finding. The relationship is one of tool to task; navigational technique is a prerequisite to route-finding. Once the initial plan is formed the adventurer runs headlong into the question of *which way* is the better way to get from A to B — safely.

Much of the knowledge that goes into making a route-finding decision can come only with experience, but we can profitably outline some of the more troublesome problems and problem areas. First a note about decision-making within a wilderness party.

Decision-Making

Within small groups of friends who share common experiences the decision-making process is and should be an informal affair. Each member is fully aware of the talents and capabilities as well as the shortcomings of his companions. When the occasion arises each will contribute from his own special areas of strength, trusting the same from the others. More often than not a sound decision will emerge, or at worst a poor judgment will be reversed before serious hardship results from it.

Among larger groups, however, or those with no common experience, or in parties with a high percentage of inexperienced members, decision-making should not be left so fully to the foibles of pure democracy. The greater the required degree of organized effort in attaining an objective, the greater is the need for a final authority. The mundane chores of planning menus, buying supplies, arranging transportation, writing equipment lists, etc., simply will not get done without an appointed leader. The same goes without elaboration for the many minor emergencies and the few genuine crises which so suddenly arise in the outdoor world.

On the other hand, one of the strengths of good leadership is the ability to delegate authority. It is important to the purpose of the outing, both aesthetic and geographic, that everyone in the group be allowed to participate and not merely asked to co-operate. Thus the appointed leader is more of an expediter-coordinator than a dictator. He must know when to command absolutely as well as unhesitatingly when to seek the advice of others. His decisions must be a consensus of group wishes and abilities, coupled with his own rational thinking.

The decision-making process itself should be a deliberate one. The factors which go into it, such as party strength, available time, equipment on hand, and so forth, have been touched upon in another context. When the occasion for a decision arises, all of these must be carefully weighed. Most often a wrong choice brings only discomfort, but the infrequent occurrence that brings tragedy is more than reason enough for intelligent handling of *every* decision point in route-finding.

High Elevation

We might arbitrarily define "high elevation" as any place over 6,000 feet, especially if it's much above one's accustomed elevation. Individuals will be affected differently according to how fast they arrive there, how well prepared they are physically, how long they stay, and what they do while there. Strenuous physical activity at high elevation gives the sportsman much to think about, and first in priority is the physiological effect of breathing rarified air.

The human respiratory system is capable of adjusting to a reasonably thin oxygen content, but the process takes time. Mountain climbers have gained the summits of most of the world's major peaks, many above 25,000 feet, without the aid of supplementary oxygen equipment. Such ascents frequently take several weeks with party members gradually exposing themselves to higher and higher elevations in establishing the final assault camp.

At 18,000 feet the atmosphere contains only one half the oxygen that it does at sea level. The strongest of individuals suddenly transported from a relatively low elevation to that height would become unconscious or at least incapacitated in a short time. Though the body requires the same amount of oxygen to perform a given chore at any elevation, the higher one goes the harder the lungs, heart, and circulatory system work to fill the need. Taken to 18,000 feet, these stalwart organs are forced to process twice the volume of air they do at sea level.

Few of us need to be concerned with such extremes of elevation, but far lower ones cause great discomfort and even death to too many sportsmen each year.

The favorite hunting, fishing, and backpacking areas of our higher western states annually record significant numbers of heart attacks among visitors from low elevations. Without a sufficient adjustment period, which is properly called *acclimatization,* a normal, healthy person will feel the effects of moderate exertion at 6,000 or 7,000 feet and experience definite breathing problems at 9,000 to 10,000. It is not at all unusual in these times of rapid travel for a man to leave a desk job in the East on Saturday and be hunting at 8,000 to 10,000 feet a day or two later. This is too much too fast.

Becoming acclimated to higher elevations requires a modification of the body's oxygen-processing machinery, specifically an increase in the number of blood cells, the red corpuscles, which load up with oxygen in the lungs and carry it to all parts of the body. The more red corpuscles, the faster the demand is met. There is no set rule on how long it takes to adjust to a change in elevation. The time period will vary with the amount of change, the degree of exertion, and to some extent on the age and physical condition of the individual. The first few days at a significantly higher elevation there is a tendency to feel dull and lazy in the normal routine of the day. Up to two weeks are required before anything like full acclimatization is achieved.

More serious than the lethargy which grips the oxygen-starved brain is the effect the depletion has on one's faculties of judgment and reasoning. As with any other pursuit, the edge of difference may show itself in an emergency. Far more often the failure to acclimatize will take its toll in low endurance and ill temper.

For those who climb really high and remain there for weeks at a time, the body protests its oxygen ration in a way to which it cannot adjust. The process of cell repair breaks down, making every small cut or scratch a serious matter. After a few weeks above 20,000 feet, normal rest and sleep become impossible and effective work is out of the question. Those who vie for summits at such elevations know that they have one or possibly two chances at the top before they must seek lower shelter.

There is only one way to become acclimated to a particular elevation and that is to live in it, taking a few days to work up to a planned level of exertion. Maintaining good physical conditioning, while no substitute, is a definite help. This means achieving the capacity for sustained physical activity *equal to or greater than* that planned at the outing site. It does not mean obtaining a doctor's pronouncement of good general health. Physical readiness will not increase the red corpuscle count, but it will strengthen chest and heart muscles and prepare them to handle larger loads on demand.

The party which does not take the time to condition itself at home will do it on the trail where it comes in massive doses. Frayed nerves, sore muscles, and general exhaustion all must be subtracted from the ledger of pleasant memories. The actual acclimatizing can only be done on the trip itself. Those who cannot plan an extra week for the purpose can make the jump a little more pleasant by taking it easy the first few days.

One of the more unpleasant manifestations of inadequate acclimatization is a malady known as "altitude sickness." When the body finds that it cannot fill all of its demands for oxygenated blood, it begins to order priorities. In order to meet the highest need of the moment it will restrict or shut off completely the supply to other areas. A prime example is the sleepiness which follows a heavy meal; the demand for blood in the digestive areas detracts from the flow to the brain with a resulting loss in efficiency. Altitude sickness is closely related but in the opposite direction. To meet the extreme physical demands of high-elevation travel, the body will restrict blood flow to the internal organs in favor of the muscles. In many individuals this disturbs the digestive organs to the point of nausea and weakness. Other symptoms are headache, shortness of breath, lack of appetite, vomiting, and insomnia. In addition to acclimatization and good physical condition, care in planning the diet can help to minimize occurrences of altitude sickness. With each increase in altitude, portions should increasingly favor carbohydrates and cut down on fatty foods. The only sure cure for the affliction, however, is immediate return to a lower altitude and complete rest.

Camp cooking, probably the butt of more jokes than any other phase of outdoor living, takes on other worries at high elevation in addition to the digestive problem discussed above. Because of unusually severe exertion, and because of the slowdown in cell replacement, a diet of wholesome, appetizing foods is more and more necessary the higher one goes. When food must be backpacked to high camp the problem is especially great, for the more nutritious and appealing foods seem also to weigh the most. Nearly all conventional foods such as fresh meats and vegetables, and canned goods of all kinds, contain too much water to be carried in any great quantity.

Modern food processing has worked some small wonders in removing water from foods with its more recent techniques of freeze-drying. The water in quickly frozen foods is evaporated directly from the solid state, leaving the cell structure, with its texture and flavor, largely intact. Good as the process is, it considerably increases the cost of the product.

The only other commercially practicable water-removing process is the widely used dehydration method. As with freeze-dried foods, dehydrated items must undergo rehydration before use. Of the two methods, dehydrated goods require much more preparation time. Beans and rice, for example, should be soaked overnight, and other vegetables take equally long. Rehydration time suggested on the package should be viewed with extreme skepticism.

Many foods which require rehydration are prepared by boiling, and this introduces another difficulty in high-elevation camping. Cooking times for boiled foods increase drastically with elevation gain. As altitude increases, atmospheric pressure decreases, and water boils at successively lower temperatures. Each 5,000-foot gain in height brings approximately a 10° drop in boiling temperature, and each 10° drop in temperature *doubles* the cooking time. Look at what this does to a "three minute" egg.

Elevation	Boiling Temp.	Cooking Time
Sea level	212°	3 minutes
5,000 feet	202°	6 minutes
10,000 feet	192°	12 minutes

A lightweight pressure cooker is an excellent investment for the party which plans on being very long at high elevations. It will save on water, fuel, and time. Without one, as the above table suggests, boiling foods at much over 5,000 feet is not very practical. A good backpacker's model is available from camping equipment suppliers.

The severity of all problems associated with high elevation takes an upward jump with the passage of the tree line. This is the rather variable line above which trees, shrubs, and all but the most hardy of plants will not grow. The world above tree line is a harsh one. Route-finding is complicated by lack of identifiable features, weather is subject to sudden and violent change, and effective shelter, if one is to be certain of having it, must be carried from lower elevations. Any time a route-finding decision will take a party onto slopes above substantial vegetation, the leader had better consider that conditions for his group's survival may become critical.

Stream Crossing

The idea of a cooling plunge into a gently flowing valley stream may have great appeal on a hot summer afternoon, but it loses something of its charm on a gray and windy fall morning when the air temperature is a frisky 25° F. Stream crossing is pleasant at best, and time-consuming as well as dangerous at its worst.

Time is conserved by choosing the crossing site as much in advance as possible. As with most route-finding problems, the distant and elevated view of the various alternatives is very helpful in making a decision. If nothing more, at least the poorest of the choices may be eliminated.

Narrowing the choices narrows the area of commitment, which implies two things: after a particular approach has been made it is no longer possible to compare the site with others; should the wrong site have been chosen, backtracking to the decision point or else bushwacking a route up or down stream to a second choice is tiring and infinitely more time-consuming.

The trusty topographic map should be the first line of offense in anticipating stream-crossing troubles. Size being equal, streams with gentle gradients will obviously be preferable to those running over steeper terrain. A gradient of ten feet per mile may be considered gentle. Where stream width is likely to make even a gentle crossing a dangerous undertaking, it may be safer to move further up the valley. Despite the increased gradient, upstream tributaries get narrower — to the point where the swiftest current may be crossed safely. Thus where the safety of a particular crossing is in doubt, the map may reveal a better gradient area or possibly an upstream branching where two tributaries can be managed more easily than the single main stream. Wherever bridging materials might be needed, the map is also useful in choosing in advance a timbered location for the attempt.

Chance plays some part in determining where a crossing can safely be accomplished. In well-forested country it is almost always possible to find large trees which have fallen across waterways. These make usable bridges over all except the widest of rivers. The less sure-footed may straddle and scoot their way across in perfect safety. More often one will find a string of stepping stones in place for a light-footed, sprinting traverse. For these it is well to pick out an entire route ahead of time and to keep the eyes several jumps ahead of the feet.

At times a *three*-legged crossing can be made in current which would sweep your two legs out from under you. For this one find a stout pole and place it firmly on the bottom on the *downstream* side. While braced with the pole, move the feet forward to stable positions on the stream floor, then move the pole quickly ahead to a new bracing stance. While the pole is out of the water the legs should be somewhat spread, one upstream and the other downstream, to hold against the current. Move with a shuffling motion, taking care to plant one foot firmly before lifting the other. In wading a current, do not lift the feet higher than necessary for moving them forward and over obstacles in the stream bed. Water flow is always fastest on a stream's surface, precisely where it can do the most to foil your balance.

A current too dangerous to free wade or swim may be tackled by a volunteer on a rope. If he can get a line across, the rest of the party may use it as a hand line.

Two other techniques which require ropes are the Tyrolean Traverse and the Burma Bridge, illustrated in *Figures 56* and *57*.

> **Figure 56.** The Tyrolean Traverse method of crossing a stream or chasm. Top two drawings illustrate two postures for use in making the crossing; the bottom one shows how inert loads can be ferried across the same fixed rope.

Figure 57. The Burma Bridge is a great deal of work to construct, but is worth the time and effort when many or repeated crossings are to be made.

The catch in either method is that one man must first be gotten across with the rope to set it up. In fairness to practice, however, it often happens as suggested above that the current will allow an unencumbered volunteer to keep his footing where it would be highly dangerous for the party to attempt it with loads. The packs and gear may then be easily sent across in Tyrolean fashion or carried over on the resulting Burma Bridge.

Occasionally the situation permits throwing the loop end of a doubled rope or even a lariat type loop in a single rope over a strategically located projection on the distant shore; possibly a short log tied into the end of a rope can be thrown and wedged among rocks or trees on the other side after the fashion of a grappling hook. Too often, though, the scene is not so handily arranged. The distant shore will be too distant, all projections will be broad and low, and probably the wind will be blowing in the wrong direction for rope throwing as well.

However the first rope is transported across, it will have to be pulled as tightly as possible and anchored securely to a tree or rock on both sides of the chasm. The Tyrolean Traverse set-up consists of a single rope thus tied. It must be suspended high enough above the water to prevent the crosser's weight from stretching the rope until he receives a dunking anyway. Ideally, unless an immediate recrossing is contemplated, it should be rigged from a high bank to a low one so that gravity will do most of the work; the crosser can then pretty much slide or push himself down the rope.

There are several methods of making the actual crossing on a Tyrolean setup, that is, of arranging the body on the rope. The easiest and fastest is that of slinging oneself sloth-like under the rope, looping the legs over the line and holding on with both hands — much in the same position as when climbing a fixed rope, but with the body horizontal rather than vertical. A second and safer approach is that of lying lengthwise on *top* of the rope with one foot hooked over it (across the instep) and the other hanging straight down. One can get onto the rope by straddling it, grasping it with both hands, then leaning forward, at the same time lifting one leg behind to hook the rope with the instep. The second leg must be kept down at all times. The crossing is much easier than it sounds since the hanging leg acts as a counterweight in keeping the trunk in balance. It is safer than the first method because in the hanging position a slip of the hands means a fall. If one does lose his balance while atop the rope he may still clutch it and go into the hanging leg-wrap position beneath it.

A third method of making a Tyrolean crossing necessitates a bit more preparation but is especially useful for transporting packs and other objects which cannot supply their own power, or for securing an individual where a fall would mean more than getting wet. The load (or the individual) is suspended from the taunt line by means of some type of hanger—a strap, a carabiner*, or anything which is strong enough and will facilitate sliding—and drawn across by means of separate draw ropes attached to the load and operated from shore. The two rope handlers take in or let out rope to ferry loads across and to return the hanger.

The Burma Bridge is a V-shaped trough constructed of at least three ropes; one rope serves as a walkway while two others, above and on either side of the first, provide handrails. The walkway

---

* A carabiner (KARE-uh-bean-er) is a metal snap-link used in a variety of ways by mountaineers. They are available from sports equipment dealers carrying climbing gear. Whatever is used, make certain it will carry the load, and inspect it frequently for excessive wear and heat damage from friction.

can be doubled for better footing, but the construction is the same. For greater stability the three strands should be laced together from hand rail to walkway to handrail, etc. The lacing may consist of lighter weight rope, either in short pieces tied in at intervals of about three feet, or as one continuous line (to save cutting a good rope). Either way it is accomplished it should be knotted each time it connects with a handrail. This will prevent excessive chaffing and wearing of the ropes.

The clove hitch is a good knot for the lacings, while the ever useful and dependable bowline is best for the tie-ins on shore.

A crossing may also be made in relative safety with only one handrail. With this setup the crosser steps sideways along the lower ropes while leaning into the single railing to prevent his flopping to the unprotected side.

It is very easy to underestimate the force of water. Where depths can be kept below knee level considerable current can be withstood. When the same or even gentler water rises to thigh or hip level two things happen; the body's natural buoyancy begins to assert itself, and the widening body gives a much greater surface for the water to push against. When judging the force of any current, pick out an object which breaks the water's surface and note the pushing effect at that point. Beware the current that piles water more than an inch or so on the upstream side of an obstruction. With strong current in evidence, a swimming crossing of a pool above or below the shallow but more dangerous area may be safer.

If crossing is essential at a place where safety is

in doubt, make the first attempt without encumbrances such as heavy clothing and backpack. As with any crossing, choose a spot just downstream of a danger point or enough upstream so that failure will not mean being swept into it.

Wet clothing is usually the most troublesome aspect of a stream crossing, both for its drag in the water and for its discomfort once out of it. Where a complete dunking is unavoidable, remove as much clothing as possible beforehand. It can be kept dry by carrying it out of the water or by using the Tyrolean method. For a cold wading, remove boots and socks, but put the boots back on for stability. Once on the other side the dry socks will be appreciated, while the boots with excess water drained out, will be damp for a while but not soggy.

Snow

Snow cover changes the character of a route in every respect. It covers tracks, trails, and trail signs. It obstructs visibility while falling, and is an obstacle while on the ground. Most of all it is evidence of an environment in which man must have special skills and equipment in order to survive. "Snow," however is many different things.

In summer, at elevations where snowfields survive until late in the season, or perhaps remain to lie under the new snows of winter, the compacted old snow may provide a welcome pavement covering brush and rougher terrain below. Summer snow does have its pitfalls though, and quite literally. Drifting new snow will tend to bridge ditches, boulders, and the lee sides of vertical obstructions, sometimes leaving air pockets of considerable size. No better tiger trap was ever devised. Other such booby traps are formed by solar radiation as it is absorbed more readily by darker objects protruding from the snow surface than by the highly reflective surface itself. Large and deep gaps form between trees or rocks and the snow around them. These also may drift over, or undercut the snow well back from the object itself.

Even more dangerous are the tunnels created by melt water running beneath heavy snow accumulations in ravines and valleys. In the spring and early summer months these become doubly dangerous as melting swells the streams to icy torrents and tunnel roofs become weaker with each passing hour. Eventually the roofs collapse of their own weight, but prior to that time often provide the only bridges over the impasse. The route-finder never knows when the addition of his own weight will place the last straw of burden on the section being crossed. With no way out of the frigid water, even if footing can be kept for a time, strength and life ebb quickly.

In recent years a double fatality occurred on the lower slopes of Mt. Rainier when a family of four shortcutted a route marked out by Rangers. The area is not glaciated but holds deep snow all summer long and is in the path of melt waters from glaciers above. Any summer snowfield will present a similar situation and should be traversed with caution.

Preparation for summer snow travel should include the carrying of at least one mountaineering rope and the knowledge of how to use it. Most large cities have mountain clubs which provide such instruction. Warm clothing and emergency overnight shelter should always be taken along by those who plan to be on snow for very long. Wherever snow can survive July and August in the mid-latitudes, it is a reasonable guess that the sun and warmtn of the daytime will quickly drop to freezing with the arrival of darkness.

The violent and dynamic precipitations of winter are a far cry from the dormant leftovers of spring and summer. Snow types run from hip-deep soft powder to unyielding frozen crust which can barely be dented by a sturdy boot toe. Each type requires a different mode of attack for travel and for making a comfortable camp.

Route-finding considerations for snow travel include skill, time, party preparedness, and special equipment. Every single act of the daily routine of eating, sleeping, and moving connected with a cold-weather outing takes much more time and energy than the same function in a milder environment. The strength-sapping cold, the encumbering heavy clothing, and the balkiness of cold-stiffened equipment make everything more difficult. All of these combine to exert an effect on will and morale that becomes a dangerous ingredient of each route-finding decision. Right choices bring only expected privations and challenging living conditions, but wrong choices — those for which party reserves of skill, time, preparedness, and equipment are not adequate — threaten life itself.

Load movement is one of the greatest problems of wilderness winter travel. The method chosen should be based on snow consistency and terrain character. Excepting the use of motorized snow vehicles, a light snow cover is best traversed on foot using adequately soled boots. For deeper snows the choice is between skis and snowshoes, each of which has its advantages and drawbacks.

Skiers choose skis to the man, while nonskiers, that is, those who are not skilled in their use, prefer snowshoes. Anyone who can walk can get by on snowshoes the first time out. The nonskier embarking on a winter trip with skis would have trouble just standing up let alone charging through virgin powder wearing a forty-pound pack. For mountain travel, the problem is compounded by having to move roped together.

The big advantage of skis is speed, of the snowshoe, maneuverability in tight places—for example, in heavy vegetation. Snowshoes are lighter and more easily carried than skis when that need arises. Another point to consider is the general cost of the equipment. Alpine ski equipment, the type owned by most skiers, is poor for cross-country travel. Ski touring requires a different ski and binding design, one which allows the heel to lift freely for walking. The cost of such special equipment is difficult to justify for occasional use. Even snowshoes, which are less expensive than skis, come in different designs for various snow and terrain conditions. Perhaps the best advice to the uninitiated is to try each method using rented equipment, then make a personal choice. Part of the preparation for any trip is in becoming familiar with all equipment prior to the time it must be depended upon.

Whether walking, skiing, or snowshoeing, you have to carry the load on your back. The only effective alternative, in gentle and open terrain, is the sled or toboggan. Two men can easily carry the load of three when sliding it across a snowy landscape. The firmer the surface, the better for such transport. Deep layers of cold, fluffy powder or soft, sticky, late-season snows will slow you down. It's wise to have packframes along just in case.

Wind, temperature, and time affect snow soon after it hits the ground, giving it a wide range of surfaces. Heavy crusts form after warming and freezing cycles or after rain. Though the sun may soften them again in the daytime, north ridges and shadowed areas often remain solid enough to support a heavy traveler. Windward or flat terrain may become wind-packed enough to walk on comfortably. Early in the morning snows may be firm, but quickly soften as afternoon approaches. A little observation and scouting may save a great deal of time and fatigue.

The primary danger of snow travel on any steep terrain comes from the ever-present possibility of an avalanche. The reasons for snow slides are many and complicated, some not yet fully understood. They involve deterioration of snow crystals, the bonding qualities of successive snow layers, temperature changes, and other factors far beyond our scope. Even the trained observer is hard pressed to predict when or if a slope will unburden itself on the valley below.

Though on-site judgments are of doubtful reliability, there are some general warning signs and traveling precautions which serve to minimize the danger of being caught in a slide path. Open, steep slopes are always subject to suspicion, especially after a recent heavy snowfall. Do not fail to consider that such slopes above seemingly protected ones may discharge with force enough to override lower barriers of forest cover. A large avalanche packs a tremendous amount of power, enough to sweep a path through large timber, cross a valley floor for long distances, and have sufficient momentum to carry hundreds or even thousands of feet up the opposing slopes.

Slides of such magnitude are not the rule, but it should be obvious that a narrow valley between steep slopes is not the safest place to be walking when snow slides are in evidence. A better choice is the ridge crest itself. If one must cross a risky-looking area, the traverse is best made high rather than low, and preferably in an area of *concave* slope. A convex slope, such as at the brow of a rise — where it begins to level off markedly — puts great surface tension on snow layers as it bends them outward. Footprints across such a stressed surface can break loose an avalanche exactly in the same way that perforations in a sheet of paper cause it to tear at that point.

Another general rule of travel in potentially dangerous terrain is that the easiest route up a slope is also the path of least resistance downward for any falling debris. Gullies and smooth, open slopes invite disaster where snow or loose rock await the last push of frost, sun, or wind that starts them down. These are nature's pathways, and man is a trespasser on them. One of the most soul-searching experiences a party can have is making the choice between the easy but dangerous way and the more difficult but safer route up or down a mountain.

Avalanche danger is greatest after heavy snowfalls, especially when there is a marked difference between the old and the new snow layers. If they fail to adhere or bond to one another, slippage can occur. Temperature changes tend to increase the instability of snow layers. It is therefore a good idea not to disturb steep snow slopes soon after freezing has begun. Until the process is well underway, freezing of the top layer creates a greater disparity between it and lower layers.

The best overt signs of avalanche danger are miniature slides themselves. The traveler may kick loose small surface slides with every step. These bear watching, though they are more unnerving than serious unless they begin to involve underlayers.

A second visible indicator of slide potential is *sun balling*. A sun ball is a small amount of sticky snow which spontaneously rolls down a steep slope, picking up material as it moves. It rarely becomes dangerous as a falling object, but a large number or their tracks is symptomatic of an overall weakness in the snow cover. Heavy, wet snow, or any snow for that matter, may reach the point where its adhesion to the slope is overcome by gravity.

The best rule of all is to avoid potentially hazardous areas when at all possible.

Glacier Travel

Glacier travel is for technically skilled and prepared parties only, and never for a party of less than three no matter how skilled and prepared.

A glacier differs from other ice and snow mainly in that it is in motion; the weight of accumulating snows in its upper reaches, combined with gravity and a steep gradient, causes its ice to flow downward. The great stresses put upon the more or less brittle material cause it to crack open along its surface. These cracks, called crevasses, reach awesome dimensions, many yards across and a hundred feet and more in depth. The dangerous ones are not the picturesque canyons visible to the most innocent novice, but the hidden ones, bridged over with a few feet of solid-looking snow. Even very large crevasses bridge over or partially fill in during winter and create a guessing game for the route-finder.

There is no objective of sport route-finding which justifies the presence of individuals or unprepared groups on a glacier.

Brush Battling

Brush battling is like any other form of combat; avoidance of the confrontation is preferable, but if that becomes impossible it is well to know something of the character of the enemy.

The makeup of brush varies with local growing conditions. Usually it is a mixture of undergrowth forms of deciduous shrubbery and tough weeds, but in harsher environments it may consist of stunted evergreens woven together in directing their scant growth outward rather than up.

As a stand of trees matures it chokes out much of the mat of young hardwoods and larger plants on the forest floor. Where conditions prevent the growth of larger species, then, brush will tend to thrive. Stream valleys, snow-slide paths, and exposed stretches subject to extreme winds and cold temperatures are typically brushy areas. Brush needs a good water supply, hence will tend to prevail on wetter western slopes or, in more arid regions, on northern slopes which are watered by heavier accumulations of winter snows.

Slide paths tend to be used several times yearly as dumping chutes for snow from higher elevations.

The larger species of forest cover on these slopes are never allowed to develop beyond the sapling stage, lying flat and impassive before the devastating assault of snow and ice. After being knocked down repeatedly, surviving specimens no longer try to grow straight and tall. The result is an unbelievable tangle of such species as alder and bowed young evergreens.

A similar state of affairs exists at the lower margin of many talus slopes. These also receive the snow burdens which cannot remain for long on steep slopes above. In other areas, such as those of the prevailing westerlies in our Northwest states, or the east-lying ridges of the Appalachian chain, the impetus is the luxuriant growing conditions brought on by abundant rainfall.

If at all practicable, such jungles of interwoven vegetation should be skirted. Depending on the nature of the trip and the location of the objective, an early-season entry may be best. In May or June it may be possible to use the troublemaking snow itself as a highway over the labyrinth for which it is to blame. At other times it may be more feasible to go the long way around. Many miles of trail are preferable to hours of futile lunging, hacking, and tightrope walking.

One general rule is to stick to the heaviest timber. In addition to the lighter underbrush, large trees tend to lose their lower branches, making passage quite comfortable. On the other hand, young, closely nestled trees present nearly as awesome a barrier as a brushy slope.

The blowdown is another natural barricade to be avoided. It is a pathway of destruction, usually in more mature timber, caused by a sudden violent gust of wind or by a severe storm. Though not of extensive proportions, blowdowns rival the most cunningly designed obstacle courses. The most likely place to find them is on windward slopes or in high notches or passes between mountains.

Man leaves his own form of blowdown in the wake of a logging operation. The obstacles here are the waste branches and tops (slash) and the havoc done to the earth by tracked vehicles. A corollary problem of the logging scene is the obliteration of trails and trail signs.

When it cannot be avoided, brush battling is just that, the battling of brush. One tramples, cuts, walks on, and pries apart the brush, but in the end it remains to be done all over again on the return.

13 / The Weather Eye

Weather is of critical importance to any outdoor activity, but particularly to those pursuits which take people more than a few hours from warmth and shelter. Accurate weather forecasting in the outdoors by an untrained individual is out of the question, but so too is the blind acceptance of whatever comes from the weather gods without even an attempt at second-guessing them. The alternative, somewhere between blind acceptance and sheer guesswork, is to develop a "weather eye" in the tradition of farmers, sailors, and other self-reliant peoples the world over.

Long before the days of global weather reporting and weather satellites, these people depended on their own observations to learn when and how the weather would change. The lore they developed is no less valid today. With a little science added, it is perhaps even more reliable.

Cultivating a weather eye consists of learning some of the fundamentals of meteorology and knowing a few of the weather's typical patterns and signs of change. The more you learn, and the more astute your observations, the more accurate will be your guesses.

What Makes Weather

At the heart of the weather-making process are differences in the density of air masses due in turn to differences in their temperatures. The sun heats the earth's blanket of air unevenly, causing the warmer masses to expand, become lighter (less dense) and thus to rise. Cooler and heavier air masses (more dense) immediately move into the void and a cycle has begun. The moving air is of course wind.

Weathermen speak in terms of low and high pressure rather than of heavy and light air masses. Since lighter air pushes downward with less force, it exerts low atmospheric pressure on the earth, and the opposite is true of heavier air. Measuring differences in atmospheric pressure is the function of the barometer, a key instrument in guessing the weather and the only one necessary for the outdoorsman-forecaster.

In its movement over land and seas, air picks up evaporated moisture. The warmer the air, the more moisture it can hold; thus at any given temperature it will reach a saturation point. As it rises into the upper atmosphere, warm air must cool. It does so at the normal rate of about $3\frac{1}{2}°F$ for every 1,000 feet. When its temperature drops below the saturation point for the amount of moisture it is carrying, some of it must condense back into liquid water droplets, which, as they become larger and larger, will eventually overcome the upward air currents and fall as rain. The several other forms of precipitation are variations of this same condensing process.

Air Masses and Weather Fronts

Air masses affecting the contiguous United States originate northward in the polar regions, southward in tropical zones, and in the two great maritime areas to the east and west, particularly westward over the Pacific Ocean. As they enter the country the polar and tropical contributions are deflected eastward by the great mid-latitude wind belt known as the Prevailing Westerlies. The colder air of the polar masses actually takes a compromise southeast course while the moist tropical air typically moves to the northeast. Daily weather maps in newspapers often show the two different masses to be on such a southeast-northeast collision course.

This is a highly simplified version of air-mass movement, but the point to be made is that most of our storms arrive from the western quadrants. The actual winds in any weather pattern may blow from any quarter since winds behave in a circular manner independent of the direction of the storm itself. Winds spawned in northern hemispheric high-pressure cells rotate in a clockwise direction while those in a low-pressure cell rotate counterclockwise. The effects south of the equator are reversed.

Figure 58. A typical frontal pattern in the United States. Other air masses enter the country from the oceans to the east and west.

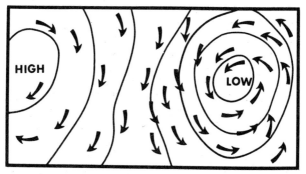

Figure 59. Wind rotation in high and low pressure cells in the Northern Hemisphere. "Highs" are associated with relatively cold air and "lows" are typically centered in relatively warm air masses. The circular lines represent the pressure gradient either increasing (high) or decreasing (low) toward the center of the cell. They are similar in function to contour lines on a topographic map.

A weather front is the leading edge of a mass of air with well-defined characteristics of density, temperature, and moisture content. More exactly, it is the meeting point between two differing masses. Since nature insists on achieving a balance, the greater these differences the more violent will be the adjustment, which of course we know as "weather."

Fronts are classed primarily as *warm* and *cold*, referring to relative differences between air masses and between ground temperatures and air masses. Each behaves in a characteristic manner, announcing its approach and passage in predictable fashion. The weather is likely to be good when either is in firm control. Here are a few general facts about each type of front:

Cold fronts. Cold air is unstable and therefore restless. Weather associated with it is often of an aggressive and violent nature, though ordinarily of shorter duration than that accompanying warm fronts. Cold air is typically clear and dry, with ceilings high and visibility good except during precipitation. A cold front moves at about 20 to 35 mph or from 500 to 700 miles per day. Because the air in a cold front is dry, thus having less extensive cloud layers, it often arrives with only a few hours' warning. The actual front may be preceded by a squall line of thunderstorms as much as 50 to 200 miles in advance. In the interim between squall line and the frontal weather itself conditions may be unsettled.

Warm fronts. Warm air contrasts with cold air in every respect. It tends to be more stable, more moist, with lower ceilings and poorer visibility even when not precipitating. Weather associated with a warm

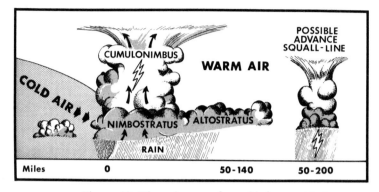

Figure 60. The advance of a cold front with its associated cloud and precipitation sequence.

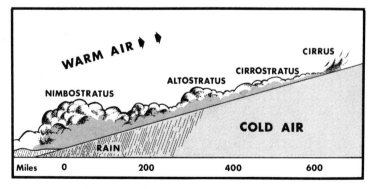

Figure 61. The advance of a warm front with its associated cloud and precipitation sequence.

front is usually limited to rain which may last several days. Clearing is typically followed by several more days of good weather. In contrast to cold fronts, warm fronts move slowly, perhaps 10 to 25 mph, or 250 to 500 miles per day. Their coming is forecast as much as two days ahead by a typical sequence of clouds and a drop in barometric pressure. Clouds and cloud sequences figure very prominently in our forecasting.

Cloud Identification

A cloud is the visible evidence of moisture content in the air. The words used to describe the different kinds of clouds may seem clumsy at first, but do not take very long to learn. Learning which name to give to which cloud, however, takes a bit more practice.

Clouds are named in three families which define their shape. *Cirrus* clouds are always high and are thin and wispy, sometimes filmlike in appearance. *Cumulus* clouds are billowy and puffy, like mounds of soapsuds. They are formed by vertical currents carrying moist air upward, and are consequently very active. They roll and surge upward and outward, changing shape in a markedly short time. *Stratus* clouds are layered. After rising moisture has begun to condense, it typically slows its vertical ascent and begins to form in horizontal or stratified layers. Cumulus and stratus clouds may form at any height, while cirrus, as noted, are always very high.

Each of the three families occur separately, but as often as not are found in combination which make identification a bit more arbitrary. Very high, puffy-looking clouds may be *cirrocumulus*, while very high, filmlike cloud sheets become *cirrostratus*. The same is true, for example, of puffy-looking clouds which are tending toward a flattish layer; these are called *stratocumulus*. There are a few more combinations, but no cloud name uses more than two of these word elements.

While the family names define cloud shape, the prefix *alto* tells us that a cloud mass is in the middle range of heights, below the cirrus family. It is used with cumulus and stratus to define middle-high *altocumulus* and *altostratus* clouds. One more designation, *nimbus*, means rain bearing. Like alto, it is used only with the cumulus and stratus family names to give us *cumulonimbus* and *nimbostratus*. You might have noticed that the order in these two is changed around a bit, but this is hardly important. Ham and eggs is the same dish as eggs and ham; the important thing is to get them both on the same plate. A third descriptive term, *fracto*, is used to denote the broken or ragged underside of a rain cloud. *Fractonimbus* is the final pronouncement that if you are not already being dripped upon, the time is near. The accompanying chart shows all of the important cloud name combinations.

		Cumulus	Stratus
Height	Cirrus	cirrocumulus	cirrostratus
	Alto	altocumulus	altostratus
Rain	Nimbus	cumulonimbus	nimbostratus

Cirrus. Highest of all clouds, like wispy locks of hair or frost patterns on a window. Often form on leading edge of warm front as it rides up over colder mass before it. Composed of ice crystals. Usually indicators of change in the weather within two days. Cirrus clouds may be the first to appear in a clear blue sky, or may appear over other forms and from a different direction.

Cirrocumulus. High, rolling, wavy groups, the true "mackerel sky." Looks like winnowed hay or gently rolling waves on the ocean. Not a frequent cloud form. Its presence is a good indicator of violent weather with the approaching front. (Distinguish carefully from *altocumulus.*)

Cirrostratus. High, whitish, filmlike sheets. Like all high clouds, *cirrostratus* never cast a shadow or completely block sun or moon. *Cirrus* generally degrade to this form rather than to mackerel sky. Due to ice-crystal content, may produce a halo of yellowish brightness around sun or moon.

Altocumulus. White to grayish rolling or scrambled patches looking like chunks of various-sized cotton. May be arranged in wavy rows and be confused with *cirrocumulus.* Puffs are larger than in the *cirro* form; they are and tend to look lower than *cirrocumulus.* If *cirrus* clouds appear in the same sky they will be an obvious overlayer to the *altocumulus* but will seem more adjacent to or grading into *cirrocumulus.* *Altocumulus* masses may produce a sun corona or disk of color around sun. The corona, formed by sunlight shining through water droplets rather than through ice crystals, is more compact than the halo of *cirro-*

Figure 62. Cirrus clouds. The larger patches are beginning to form cirrostratus sheets. Upper air conditions here are cold but relatively stable, otherwise wind currents would roll or chop the layers into cirrocumulus scrolls. Rain or snow is not far off with a sky like this.

Figure 63. Classic cumulus clouds. A "fair weather" sky from which afternoon thunderstorms occasionally develop.

Figure 64. Altocumulus or stratocumulus, depending on their height. These clouds might thicken and lower to become nimbostratus.

stratus, seeming to replace the body rather than ring it. The corona is more highly colored, ranging from pale yellow in the center to bluish or reddish edges.

Stratocumulus. Masses of spread out and flattening *cumulus* clouds in a layered formation. Not usually rain bearing, but may close to form *nimbostratus.*

Altostratus. Gray, layered mass. Blocks sun and moon but occasionally lets them peak through between thicker areas. Usually drop precipitation beginning as drizzle.

Stratus. The single family name of stratus is given to low continuous gray masses which may hang on for days producing only drizzle at the most. Uniform appearance indicates lack of internal vertical motion which is necessary for formation of raindrops of any larger size.

Nimbostratus. Precipitating low, thick, layered mass, the true rain cloud. Completely blocks sun and moon. Often present ragged or *fracto* undersides as rain falls on somebody else.

Figure 65. Nimbostratus underside with cumulonimbus tops. The leading edge of the tallest tower on the right is developing a perfect anvil associated with the final stages of a cumulonimbus "thunderhead." Rain is falling from the tower, possibly accompanied by lightning.

Figure 66. A typical combination of altostratus (*upper left*) and lower, dark masses of nimbostratus clouds. These often signal the approach of a warm front, though are not usually in such close proximity when so associated. The small dark patches are "scud" clouds, which frequently accompany nimbostratus when wind is a factor in the coming storm.

Cumulus. Puffy, billowy, white clouds with flat, grayish bottoms. These are fair-weather clouds which form on warm afternoons as sun heats the earth, forcing moistened air to rise. Cumulus clouds usually dissipate with cooling of evening, but may develop into towering *cumulonimbus*. Clouds given the family name of *cumulus* tend to be large and distinctive. In combination with other forms the *cumulus* puffiness is retained, but the individuality is lost.

214

Cumulonimbus. Towering cumulus thunderheads, often with visible anvil-shaped tops and dark, boiling underreaches. Upper fringes develop brilliantly defined outlines as interiors darken. Tremendous internal vertical air currents may reach speeds of 200 mph. *Cumulonimbus* clouds unleash thunder, lightning, rain, hail, or snow flurries on the earth. These violent activities often appear to come from *altostratus* or *nimbostratus* cloud cover just in advance of the front, but are generated by cumulonimbus above them.

The Barometer

Barometers are of two types. The mercurial barometer consists of a glass tube which is closed at the top and filled with mercury. The open end curves upward and is exposed to atmospheric pressure. High pressure pushes the column of mercury up the tube, while low pressure lets it back down. Pressure is expressed in inches of mercury.

The *aneroid* barometer contains a vacuum chamber which is depressed by high atmospheric pressure or allowed to expand by low pressure. A gearing mechanism moves a needle across a measuring scale. For convenience the scale is also expressed in inches.

Either type of barometer may be used to make weather observations, but each has some special advantages. The mercurial barometer is not meant to be moved about and is better suited for use in a laboratory or weather station. Some are owned by serious amateur weather enthusiasts. The aneroid type is less accurate than its mercurial forebear, but has the distinct advantage for our needs of being more durable and consequently more portable. It is also less expensive. One of the main reasons we shall use it is that with the addition of a second scale on its face, the aneroid barometer becomes an *altimeter*.

Any barometer registers a normal atmospheric pressure change if moved from one elevation to another. At 10,000 feet above sea level normal pressure is ten inches *less* than at the ocean surface. This breaks into the convenient figure of ¹/₁₀ of an inch (.10) for every 100 feet of elevation change.

When manufactured as an altimeter the aneroid barometer is generally more compact than in home barometer form. In the pocket watch style such as the one shown in *Figure 67*, it easily withstands being crammed into pocket or pack and carried about from place to place. Because of the small space available on the face of an altimeter, there is some problem in reading it for atmospheric pressure. The one in the photo is marked off in 100-foot intervals with a tickmark for each ¹/₁₀ of an inch. The same space on a home barometer would be expanded to include ten spaces representing hundredths of inches, and thus be more easily read for fine changes. With practice the eye can split the distance on the altimeter scale to within two or three hundredths of an inch of accuracy.

In general, when read at any one location or elevation, a rising altimeter (falling barometer) indicates deteriorating weather; and a falling altimeter (rising barometer) indicates improving weather. Though we cannot overly rely on such generalizations, they do provide a framework from which to note exceptions. Another more reliable generalization is that weather associated with a rapid barometric change is most

Figure 67. A pocket altimeter, which is also an
aneroid barometer. This one shows a reading of
approximately 3,400 feet of altitude.

often not of long duration. For example, a fast rise
after a storm may foretell a second storm close on the
heels of the first, rather than quick clearing. By the
same yardstick, a storm arriving after plunging readings may be a brief though violent one. On the other
hand, slow change usually brings conditions which
last a while, be they favorable or unfavorable.

Setting and Using the Altimeter

Like any barometer, the altimeter must be adjusted
to current atmospheric pressure in the place in which
it is to be used. There will be some type of setscrew
on the back for the purpose. All weather and radio
stations report pressure as adjusted to sea level, so
no correction is necessary for site elevation relative

to the elevation of the reporting station. At or near the trail beginning, obtain a current barometric pressure reading and rotate the needle via the setscrew to correspond. This puts the instrument in tune with what the local weather is going to do, though one cannot tell this from a single reading. While still in touch with civilization, daily forecasts are by far the best source. The barometer will not be of use until its direction and rate of change has been observed.

The adjustment to sea-level pressure should be the only internal setting necessary while in that broad area. Technically the adjustment should be carried out each time the instrument is moved upward or downward in altitude, but it will be far more practical to do this on paper. The internal setting must also be left alone so that you can observe changes in elevation, an important aspect of route-finding in itself. Pressure as well as elevation will change as the party moves, but by keeping track of readings along with actual map elevation, the navigator will know how much to attribute to elevation change and how much to the weather situation. We will look at an example a bit later.

All altimeters have one other setting mechanism, a frontal dial, which is used to turn the needle to the true elevation of a given site. This does not change the internal setting. After making the inner adjustment, rotate the outer dial until the needle rests on the correct elevation figure. This may be determined from a topographic map any time the party's point position is known.

While stationary, any change in the altimeter reading will be due to changing weather conditions, but on the trail things are a bit more complicated. For use as an altimeter alone we expect the needle to rise a certain amount as we climb or to fall a certain amount as we descend. If it changes more or less than the expected amount, when checked against a known elevation figure, we deduce that the weather is responsible for the difference. To keep track of barometric pressure at sea level, as we must for our weather watch, we look for the following relationships:

• An excessive rise on the altimeter when carried upward in elevation indicates a drop in barometric pressure of more than $1/10$ of an inch per 100 feet.

• An insufficient rise (when carried upward) indicates a drop in barometric pressure of less than $1/10$ of an inch per 100 feet.

In each case the difference from what we expect between known elevations is the important factor. Of course, a similar set of opposites is noted when coming down from one elevation to another.

Here is a sample of observations one might make while using the altimeter as both route-finding tool and weather forecaster:

Date	Time	Altimeter	Known Elevation	Barometric Pressure	Change Due to Weather
Aug. 9	9:00 pm	2600 ft.	2600 ft.	30.20 S	− −
Aug. 10	6:00 am	2600 ft.	2600 ft.	30.20 S	− −
"	10:00 am	3300 ft.	?	?	?
"	4:00 pm	3950 ft.	3900 ft.	30.15 F	−.05
"	8:00 pm	4000 ft.	3900 ft.	30.10 F	−.05

On the 9th the party camped at the trail head, setting its altimeter to a radio weather report of 30.20 S (thirty and twenty hundredths inches and steady). The map showed an elevation of 2,600 feet. Next

Figure 68. WEATHER-EYE CHART

BAROMETER READING CORRECTED	BAROMETER ACTION	WIND DIRECTION	
		NW Quadrant	**SW** Quadrant
30.20 OR HIGHER	RISING	CONTINUED FAIR FOR 24 HOURS Lower temperatures	CONTINUED FAIR FOR 12 HOURS
	STEADY	CONTINUED FAIR FOR 48 HOURS No decided change in temperature	CONTINUED FAIR FOR 12 HOURS No decided change in temperatures
	FALLING	CONTINUED FAIR FOR 24 HOURS Slowly rising temperatures	FAIR FOR 6 TO 12 HOURS Rising temperatures
30.20 TO 29.80	RISING	FAIR FOR 48 HOURS Lower temperatures	FAIR FOR 48 HOURS Lower temperatures
	STEADY	CONTINUED RAINY CONDITIONS	FAIR FOR 12 HOURS No decided change in temperatures
	FALLING	FAIR FOR 12 TO 24 HOURS No decided change in temperature	RAIN IMMINENT
29.80 OR LOWER	RISING	CLEARING WITHIN A FEW HOURS Lower temperatures	CLEARING WITHIN 6 HOURS
	STEADY	CONT'D THREATENING WEATHER Lower temperatures	CONTINUED STORMY WEATHER
	FALLING	CHANGING WEATHER	INCREASING RAIN Clearing within 12 hours

morning the altimeter reading was the same. Atmospheric pressure had remained steady overnight. At 10:00 a.m. somewhere on the trail the instrument read 3,300 feet. No map determination of elevation was made. To this point then, no check on atmospheric pressure change due to the weather alone was possible. The assumption would have to be that pressure was still steady and that the elevation of the site of the reading was truly 3,300 feet above sea level.

At 4:00 p.m. the party arrived in its camp for the night, a spot known to sit at 3,900 feet. The altimeter reading, however, was 3,950 feet, thus the altimeter had risen 50 feet *in excess* of the true elevation indicating a corresponding drop in atmospheric pressure of .05 inches. (Remember the rule of .10 inches for each 100 feet of change.) Later the same evening

WIND DIRECTION

SE Quadrant	NE Quadrant	
FAIR WEATHER	CLEAR AND COOL	This chart is for average wind velocity of 10 miles per hour.
RAIN WITHIN 24 TO 48 HOURS	CONTINUED FAIR Lower temperatures	Velocity of wind indicates speed and severity of approaching storm.
RAIN WITHIN 12 HOURS Wind increasing force . . . rising temp.	RAIN WITHIN 24 TO 48 HOURS	The speed of storm's approach and its intensity is indicated by rate of fall of barometer.
FAIR	CLEAR WITH COLDER WEATHER	
RAIN WITHIN 12 TO 24 HOURS	NO CHANGE	This chart for use only in continental United States and Canada.
RAIN WITHIN 6 TO 12 HOURS Wind increasing force . . . rising temp.	RAIN WITHIN 12 HOURS	
CLEARING WEATHER	CLEARING AND COOLER	
CONTINUED RAIN OR NO CHANGE	RAINY WEATHER Clearing 12 to 24 hours	
SEVERE STORM IMMINENT Clearing within 24 hours	HEAVY RAIN Severe north east gale colder	Courtesy of the Airguide Instrument Company, Chicago, Illinois.

NOTE:

a second reading revealed a further drop of .05 inches at the same rate of fall.

The rate of change is significant. Forecasters speak in terms of "slowly" and "rapidly." A rapid change is defined as a difference of .05 inches to .09 inches in three hours or less, so the change noted by the above party would have to be called slow.

The barometric pressure readings of 30.15 F (falling) and 30.10 F were obtained by subtracting the two .05 inch drops from previously known readings. With the latest observation at 8:00 p.m. the party had a good approximation of what the radio station back in town would be reporting that evening.

Taking the sample one step further, the party weatherman might use the Weather Eye Chart in *Figure 68* to make a guess on the nature of the coming change based on the altimeter's behavior and wind direction. These observations, together with a continual eye on the clouds, will help to keep the party aware of probable deteriorations in the weather picture as much in advance as possible.

Approach of a Cold Front

Having dealt with the barometer and with types of clouds, we can tie all together by talking about the sequence of events typically associated with arriving bad weather. Most storms are closely enough allied with weather fronts that by watching the front we can pretty much predict the coming weather. Fronts vary and change constantly within themselves, but often retain a definite identification.

Cloud sequences in a cold front

Altostratus 2–4 hours in advance, then nimbostratus, possibly preceded by cumulonimbus.

Conditions

Barometer drops (altimeter rises) steadily then rapidly as front arrives. Temperature falls. Winds from N or NW quadrant shifting to S or SW.

Description

Cold air on the leading edge of the front slides under the warmer mass ahead of it causing a rapid rise and cooling of the warm air's moisture content. Resulting altostratus clouds appear first on W or NW horizon. Rain begins, perhaps as a steady drizzle, then heavier as clouds lower and thicken to nimbostratus. Particularly fast-moving fronts will be signaled by cumulus cloud forms along with the stratus layers. These foretell gusty winds and possibly thunder and lightning with more severe forms of precipitation. Cumulonimbus clouds may be hidden from view above the stratus clouds, or precede the front by 50 to 200 miles as a squall line. If they appear in advance, the barometer will show a quick drop then steady before dropping again with the approach of the front. Cloud conditions in between will typify unsettled skies.

As the center of the disturbance arrives over the observer, the barometer will hit its lowest point and begin to rise. This low extreme is referred to as the "trough." With its passage, winds shift back around to the W or NW, the temperature falls, and the sky begins to clear. Broken masses of cumulus and cumulonimbus clouds may bring occasional showers as skies remain unsettled for a time. Settling is indicated by formation of stratocumulus bands, then higher altocumulus clouds as the cover breaks and lifts. If no further disturbance is near, clearing will follow.

Approach of a Warm Front

Cloud sequences in a warm front
cirrus up to 48 hours in advance
cirrostratus
altostratus
nimbostratus
As with the cold front, any cumulus cloud forms appearing in the sequence warn of more violent weather with the coming rains.

Conditions
Barometer drops (altimeter rises) slowly. Temperature rises. Visibility is poor with fog, haze smoke, and lowering ceilings. Winds light to calm.

Description

Warm fronts are signaled as much as 48 hours in advance by high, thin, innocuous-looking cirrus clouds formed as the leading edge of warm air rides up over the colder mass ahead of it. Cirrus wisps join to form milky cirrostratus sheets, then thicken and lower to become darkening altostratus bands. Rain begins and increases with the formation of nimbostratus layers. The barometer continues its slow decline. With passage of the front pressure begins a slow rise, while alto and nimbostratus clouds hang on for one, two, or even more days. Clearing typically lasts a corresponding period before arrival of the next front.

Many things can happen to modify the "typical" sequence of events with any type of front. Only the gathering of widespread and numerous, as well as frequent, reports can hope to keep up with the whims of such a vast and dynamic force. One confusing variation in weather patterns is the *occluded front.* An occlusion occurs when two air masses of similar disposition trap a smaller and different mass between them. The associated weather usually has characteristics of a cold front, that is, gusty and violent, but the sequence of activities will seem haphazard to the weather eye.

A second frontal event which tends to complicate weather guessing is the *stationary front.* For one reason or another an air mass may camp in an area for days or even weeks. In this case the barometer might serve to notify when a change is finally forthcoming, but be of little use in the jockeying back and forth from storm to clearing and more of each. Air, like people with nothing to do, often gets into trouble.

Other Old (Semi-) Reliable Weather Signs.

Each of the following has some basis in fact, though like most wise old sayings, exceptions occur often enough to keep one guessing.

Bad-weather indicators
• A ring around the sun or moon means rain or snow (*see* cirrostratus in Cloud I D).
• Wind-shifts from N to W then S are often accompanied by rain.
• Unusual sky tints — green, yellow, dark red or gloomy blue — bring rain and/or wind.
• Small inky clouds bring rain.
• "Red sky in the morning, sailor take warning. Red sky at night, sailor's delight."
• Clouds hanging on the heights indicate wind and rain unless they lift by midday.
• Scud clouds (small, dark, scurrying cumulus types) sweeping beneath a dark stratus layer mean that wind and rain may be near. If above the stratus layer, which may be difficult to determine, there will be wind only.
• Cloud layers moving in different directions foretell a change in wind direction corresponding to that of the upper layer.

Fair-weather indicators
• A gray dawn means fine weather.
• Fog in the valleys will burn off and clear.
• Rain rarely falls after dew forms.
• Cumulus clouds, especially those found on

bright sunny days, mean fair weather unless they tower and flatten on top.

• Red sky in the evening means a fine, generally hot, next day. Wind shifts from S to W to N are often accompanied by clearing.

Change, rather than the exact form it will take, is what the weather forecaster is concerned with. For route-finding decision-making this in itself may be enough. Rather than planning activities on the basis of what the weather *will* be, decisions can be based on what the worst *might* be. The weatherman in a party of mountain climbers might say, "There's a cold front on its way. I don't like the idea of being caught on the exposed west face in lightning. Let's do the east ridge and hope to beat the weather." Or perhaps after three wet days in a cheerless hunting camp a weather prophet might announce to his companions, "Indications are for clearing in twelve to eighteen hours. Let's wait one more day before giving up."

Of course we weren't there for the reply, but one of the others might have said, "That's what you said Tuesday."

14 / Route Finding with Aerial Photographs

A subject which is novel, fascinating, and informative should be an easy one to lead into, but aerial photography suffers the problem of being very little known and only by its professional reputation at that. The words "aerial photography" tend to evoke visions of highly skilled technicians performing complicated and precise tasks with material which would mean little to the layman. This is certainly true in some contexts, but not at all for the sporting use of air photos.

An aerial photograph, after all, is different from a casual snapshot only in that it is taken looking straight down and from a much higher vantage point. While these two exaggerated dimensions do cause a few interpretation problems at first, the user soon learns to recognize objects and topographic features by their appearances from above just as he once did from the more horizontal ground level. Photos shot over wilderness terrain may take a little more effort to read than those exposed over settled areas, but the important point is that anyone can do it, with very little special skill or equipment, but with tremendous profit in terms of route information and pre-trip pleasure. The same endless wonder of having a window seat on an airplane is found on the gound through the medium of air photos.

Aerial photography became a well developed military art during World War II, but since that time has found extensive application in many phases of the domestic scene. With a peacetime emphasis on world-wide mapping and navigation the entire United States (as well as Canada) and a large part of the rest of the free world has been photographed from the air. Much of this exciting route-finding material is available to the public.

Following World War II as well was a great increase in the number of outdoorsmen who sought their hunting, fishing, climbing, and general adventuring in the remote corners of the world. Many expeditions were led into areas for which poor maps or no maps at all existed. Aerial photography proved itself a great route-finding aid in these larger undertakings. With the expanding amount of leisure and affluence of the 1950s and 1960s it became possible for significant numbers of sportsmen to lead their own mini-expeditions to seldom visited places, and again air photos proved their usefulness.

Although this graphic route-finding tool has not yet come into frequent usage—possibly because the average wilderness traveler does not *know* about it — there is no reason it cannot be used to good advantage by anyone planning an off trail adventure, regardless of its extent. A half-inch wrench is just as useful for a battery change as it is for an engine overhaul; likewise, the navigator out for a week's sojourn in the North Cascades may have the same need for accuracy as his counterpart on a three-month Himalayan expedition.

Surprisingly easy to use, aerial photographs provide hours of valuable pre-trip study of the area of interest, and become even more valuable in the field where they can be compared first hand to the ground they represent.

Photos vs. Maps

For all of its worth a photograph does not replace a map, not even a poor one. Rather, it makes an excellent partner, supplying information the map cannot give and supporting what it can. In turn, a good map is the best aid in making the most of what is found on an aerial photograph. This rather Jack Sprat-and-wife relationship underscores a fundamental difference between the two; a map *generalizes* detail and is *selective* about how much it shows, while a photograph, for better or for worse, faithfully reproduces all that is visible from the air.*

The amount of detail needed, and thus the relative usefulness of map or photo, depends somewhat on the particular route-finding job at hand. Most

---

* The terms *selection* and *generalization* of map detail are explained in Chapter 6, Maps and Map Reading.

often a navigator works with both, much as a painter works with brushes of different sizes on the same job. The navigator takes his bearings and over-all orientation from the topo map, but turns to the aerial photograph to learn such things as the exact pattern of vegetation cover, the full detail of the lake shoreline, and the surface texture of the ground *in between* those ten-, twenty-, or forty-foot contour lines.

But photography brings more than an increase of detail to route-finding tools. Where a map is symbolic, that is, its representation is by means of lines and symbols on a more or less blank background, a photograph is a two-dimensional image of the real thing. The advantage is one of vividness, rather like the difference between the work of a portrait camera and the average untrained artist's drawing of a human face. The camera, of course, adds the wrinkles, dimples, shadows, and lines to the usual outline of eyes, nose, and mouth. In an aerial "portrait" of the land, the wrinkles are the brush patches, the rocky outcroppings, the varied stream widths, and the small woodland clearings which most often cannot be shown on even the best of maps.

The map-photo partnership is also illustrated by some pluses which fall to the map's advantage. The map is much needed for learning the true geographical orientation of each photograph. Further, there is just no substitute for the written information found on maps — the place names, the feature names, and all of the explanatory aids in the margin. Perhaps most important among the last is the map's relatively accurate scale.

It is also possible for a photograph to show *too*

much detail, or possibly only too much of one kind. Excess foliage may hide surface detail such as trails, small buildings, fading old roads, etc., which are easily portrayed on a map if known. Cloud cover, should there be any at all on the day of the filming, will block out patches of the terrain completely.

The latter observations make it clear that some judgment as to area and purpose must be used in purchasing photos. In areas of flat featureless terrain or those largely unbroken by deciduous forest they will be of limited value. In other areas they will be well justified for uses involving a vivid, in-depth look at selected areas.

When used in areas for which maps are not to be had, then, aerial photographs are a must, and when used in areas for which maps do exist, they are an excellent supplemental route-finding tool. Anyone planning an off-trail venture into country *unknown to him* should consider giving them a try.

Facts About Aerial Photography

Aerial photography is of two basic types named according to the angle at which the camera is aimed from the aircraft. A *vertical* photo is exposed as straight down from the plane as possible, while others, for technical reasons, are taken with sufficient angle to include the horizon in each print. Vertical photography is by far the most common on the domestic scene and the better for our purpose, so is the only type we shall consider in this chapter.

Photos are "flown" in batches called *projects* or *missions*. The individual exposures in each project are taken according to a definite plan. A pilot flying a particular assignment will ordinarily approach the target area from east or west (to keep all shadows in the same alignment) and take a *flight-line* of pictures along one edge. He then makes a 180° turn and approaches from the opposite direction to expose a second and adjacent flight-line. The process is repeated until the project area is covered.

Each of the resulting photographs, most commonly 9-by-9 inch contact prints, receives a unique number which is used for filing and general reference. Here is a typical numbering system, though others are used: AJB − 5T − 108.

The first group is the project or mission number, the second is the flight-line number, and the last is the individual number of one print in the sequence. With the aid of an index the user can pinpoint exactly where such a photo was taken.

The speed of the aircraft and the timing of each exposure are carefully controlled to obtain an overlap of 60 percent from one photo to the next. This is necessary if the photos are to be studied by any stereoscopic means. In addition to the forward overlap, the pilot sidelaps the flight-line by about 30 percent so that no gaps in coverage can occur in any direction.

The scale of an aerial photograph − its size in relation to the amount of area it covers − is determined by the focal length of the camera and the flying height of the aircraft when exposures are made (*Figure 69*). Suppliers will ordinarily be able to tell the buyer what scales they have before a purchase is decided upon. Though it is of limited use in distance measure, photo scale is handy as a reference for

Figure 69. Flying height affects the amount of ground covered by each photo and also the image size of objects on the film. High-flown photos mean more area but smaller detail than low-flown photos.

ordering purposes. Photo scales, which run from about 1:10000 (relatively large) down to 1:66000 and smaller, can be considered as large or small in exactly the same sense as map scale. Just remember that large scale means large detail, though less area covered per print, and that small scale means correspondingly small detail, but with a greater area of coverage per print.

The scale one chooses to purchase is important for two opposing reasons. Large-scale prints are definitely superior for route-finding uses, but conversely their cost will be greater since it will take more of them to cover the same area. From the author's point of view, however, it is easy to rationalize away the economic objection to large-scale prints. Their cost will be a small part of the expense of the usual wilderness trip. Then too, the saving in purchasing fewer but less readable small-scale work may well be false economy indeed.

If for any reason photos of unknown scale are encountered, their scale can be computed by forming a ratio between photo distance and map distance. For this it will be necessary to locate at least two points on the map which can be identified on the corresponding photo. Measure the distance on each source in inches, then form a ratio problem using this formula:

Photo scale reciprocal* =
$$\frac{\text{map scale reciprocal} \times \text{map distance}}{\text{photo distance}}$$

Here is an example: We know a particular map scale to be 1:24000, and measure two photo images to be 4 inches apart. The distance between the same points on the map is 1.5 inches. Therefore:

---

*A scale reciprocal is the denominator of the representative scale fraction. In the scale 1:62500, 62,500 is the reciprocal. See chapter 6 for a fuller discussion of scale.

$$\text{photo scale reciprocal} = \frac{24000 \times 1.5''}{4''}$$

$$\text{photo scale reciprocal} = \frac{36,000''}{4''}$$

photo scale reciprocal = 9,000

Photo scale is thus equal to 1:9000.

Other important considerations in ordering are the year and season in which the photos were taken. As far as date is concerned, current photos are probably more important than up-to-date maps, while the season in which they were flown greatly affects their readability. Much aerial photography is flown in the early spring or late fall to minimize foliage and snow cover. Some is flown at the height of the growing season so that crops or foliage are at their maximum. Under some climatic conditions missions are flown in the season of minimum cloud cover, and so on. In general, spring and fall dates will be the best for route-finding purposes.

How to Obtain Aerial Photographs

Ordering and receiving air photos takes considerable time. At least *six months* in advance, or when the first gleam of a wilderness trip appears in the mind's eye, write to the Map Information Office, U.S. Geological Survey, Washington, D.C. 20242, and request their free publication entitled *Status of Aerial Photography*. This will show available photo coverage for the entire United States and supply either the government agency holding the negatives or the fact that they are held by a private firm.

If held by a private firm, you will first have to write the Map Information Office for the name and address of the holder. All requests for photo information should be accompanied by a detailed description and sketch of the desired area of coverage. Once the holder of the film is known, write to that party and request information regarding scale, price, and dates available.

Some agencies may refer the buyer to an *index mosaic* for the actual ordering. A mosaic is a composite photograph of all photos in an area, printed at a small enough scale to allow putting it on a single map-sized sheet of paper. Each index, which usually costs about $1.50, will contain all necessary ordering information.

Holding agencies ordinarily keep only negatives on file, so all print orders they receive must be specially made up. This takes much time beyond the initial correspondence, so again, start early and always supply the most complete information possible as to just what is needed.

Aerial photographs of Canadian territory may be obtained from the Air Photographic Unit, Department of Energy, Mines, and Resources, Ottawa, Canada.

Handling Your Photos

The day the package arrives is like Christmas morning, but do not allow your new toys to become spread all over the house before taking inventory. Arrange the prints sequentially and check to see that everything ordered has been sent. Supplying agencies handle a great many such requests, and some errors are inevitable.

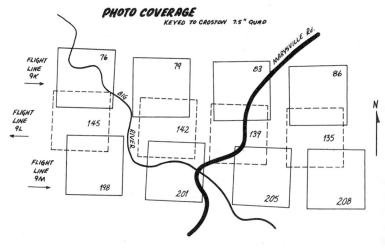

Figure 70. A working index of photo coverage. This one represents about forty 9″ x 9″ aerial photographs.

If only a few photos are involved, say a dozen or so, no special filing or handling technique is called for; each print will soon become familiar enough to be easily located. With larger orders, though, a more organized approach is necessary, and the best of these is to construct a *photo coverage overlay.*

An overlay is a piece of transparent material such as clear plastic, acetate, or tracing paper on which the border outline of every third or fourth print in each flight-line has been drawn. While being constructed, or later for use in pulling out the desired print, the overlay is repositioned on the appropriate map. In this way the outline of each photo is made to correspond with its area of coverage on the map.

A sample photo coverage overlay appears in *Figure 70.* As in the illustration, start at either end

237

of a flight-line with a single photo and choose three to five clearly identifiable points in its corners or along its edges. These same points located on the map will define that photo's area of coverage. Draw a square on the overlay for the first and last photos in each flight-line, then for each third or fourth one in between. Clearly label each photo with its individual number, and print the flight-line number out to one side. Alternate flight-lines should be done in different colors or broken lines to keep them separated.

After a few photos have revealed the standard area of coverage, make a cardboard template and use it to trace in the remaining boxes. Once the template has been cut only two to three points per photo need be located, and the work will go much faster. Exactness of boundaries is not critical since photos and flight-lines overlap as much as they do.

To help in keying the overlay to the map, trace in several prominent features such as a river, a highway or two, or the shoreline of a large lake. When the overlay is called for this added detail will help to reposition it quickly, and a glance will tell within a photo or two the exact print number to select from the stack. Keeping prints in numerical order also speeds retrieval.

Every time the photos are used you will be glad all over again for having made the photo coverage overlay.

When not in use aerial photographs should be kept out of the light and away from extremes of temperature and humidity. They have a tendency to curl if not stored in a flat position with a slight amount of pressure on them.

Viewing Aerial Photography

The viewing and studying of an aerial photograph can be as simple as looking at a snapshot. By ordering every other print in a flight-line continuous coverage can still be had with only half the expense. Single photos can be studied with the aid of a low-powered magnifying glass or even with the naked eye with good results. To get the most out of the material, however, stereo viewing is a must.

Human vision yields a three-dimensional effect because the two eyes actually view an object from different positions.* Adjacent photographs in a flight-line make a *stereo pair* because they simulate this slightly different angle of view. The hitch is that to be seen in three dimensions the images on the two photos must be relayed to the brain as separate but *simultaneous* views, one by each eye. The brain will then fuse them together into one stereoscopic whole.

The immediate aim of any stereo viewing technique is to prevent the eyes from converging on one or the other of the photos in the pair. There are a couple of uncomplicated ways of doing this, and as usual, the better one involves the expense of obtaining a hand stereo viewer or *stereoscope* such as the one shown in *Figure 71*. It consists of two lenses, each of which directs one eye to one photo.

---

*Human vision is actually *two* dimensional. Depth cues, which are learned, add the third dimension. To prove this, hold a hand over one eye and look around; breadth of field is lost, but objects are still seen in three dimensions with the lone eye.

Like reading glasses, the stereoscope must be adjusted until its lenses are the same distance apart as the observer's eyes. All models are easily set by means of a sliding bar connecting the eye pieces. This adjustment can be made by an accurate measurement of one's inter-pupilary distance, but is adequately found by experimenting with different settings; the one which feels most comfortable optically is the one to use.

For the first attempts at stereo viewing, pick out a pair of adjacent photos having the same clearly defined image somewhere near the photo centers. A building, a tower, or a distinctive landform is best because of its vertical prominence, and images closest to the centers of the photos will suffer the least amount of image displacement. (We shall explain image displacement on page 244.)

Place the stereo pair on a flat surface in an over-lapped position with about $2\frac{1}{2}$ inches between identical images. Always point the shadows of hills, buildings, trees, etc., toward the observer, otherwise depressions and projections may seem to be reversed. This effect can be observed in *Figure 72*. With the book right side up the dominant landform in the picture appears for what it is—a long snow-covered ridge. With the book turned upside down it tends to look more like a high snow-covered plateau ending in an abrupt escarpment.

With the stereoscope directly over the images peer through the lenses. If the images are not fused into one, as they almost certainly will not be at first, slide the top photo in or out until the images appear to float toward one another. When properly aligned —and the normal convergence of the eyes has been

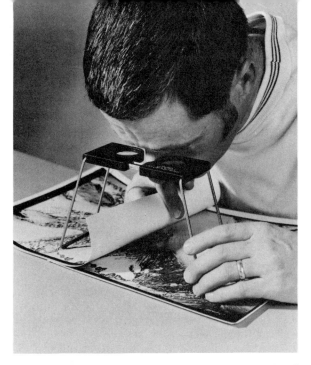

Figure 71. Using a stereoscope to view a pair of aerial photographs. One hand moves the top photo as required while the other holds the instrument in place.

overcome—the stereo effect will "pop" into being. Some persons see stereo immediately, but most spend a few minutes at it. A very few individuals do not have stereo capability due to their own ocular defects.

Depending upon where the image is located relative to the edge of the print, the edge may have to be curled upward out of the way. This causes a bit of a handling problem at first until one learns to move the viewer, curl and slide the top photo, and keep everything coordinated.

A second method of obtaining the stereo effect uses no viewer but does involve foiling the tendency of the eyes to converge. This one takes a bit more practice because the eyes must be trained to do all of the work. Eye divergence is aided by a physical barrier rather than being forced by lenses.

Cut a piece of cardboard about 6-by-8 inches and, after laying out a stereo pair of photos as in *Figure 71,* place the divider long way up between the photos. Resting the forehead and nose squarely along the cardboard, look directly down on the images and move the top photo in or out until the images appear to fuse. This method is considerably more difficult to master, yet professional photo handlers soon learn to see stereo even without barriers or lenses of any sort. It is all a matter of training the muscles of the eyes.

Whether using the viewer or the cardboard divider method, the biggest part of the trick is to look through rather than at the photo surfaces. If the stereo effect is slow to come, stare at a more distant point for a few seconds, then, holding the stare, look back at the images.

The habit of forcing the eyes to diverge rather than converge as normal might seem to be harmful to them, but this is apparently not true. Persons who work constantly with stereo viewing devices suffer no ill effects other than expected eye fatigue.

Most stereo pairs of photographs yield an exaggerated account of terrain relief. Through the viewer gentle slopes become steep hills and steep hills become terrifying precipices. The exaggeration is purposefully built in by lengthening the distance between photo exposures, sort of like

Figure 72. Aerial photographs should be viewed with shadows toward the observer. The photo number, in white ink, is upside down. Try looking at this mountain ridge from both directions.

separating the eyes by an extra foot or so. This is necessary because aerial views understandably tend to flatten terrain features. After an experience or two with terrain-to-photo comparison, the route-finder will know how to evaluate the vertical exaggeration. With the first order one might try getting a few pairs of photos taken over an area of familiar ground. These provide excellent training in all aspects of photo identification.

Photo Scale in Distance Measure

Aerial photographs occasionally must be used without the help of a map. As variable as photo scale is it must then be used for what it is worth—a very rough guide to ground distance. The reason for this unreliability points out yet another difference between map and photo.

Unlike a map, a photograph is a reproduction of what can be seen from a single viewing position, the position of the lens at the center of the print. Slight distortions occur as a result of lens quality, and even more because of the same illusion which makes parallel lines appear to us to converge in the distance, but these are insignificant compared to the *image displacement* illustrated in *Figure 73*. Any vertical feature, whether a landform or a building, will be imaged *away* from the optical center of a photograph. The greater the distance from the center and the taller the feature, the greater will be the displacement. Only at photo center will the scale hold relatively true.

The smoke stacks in *Figure 73* are supposedly equidistant from one another. The camera angle, however, shows only one of them in the vertical perspective which preserves true scale. The others, from right to left, appear to lean increasingly outward, and the view is more and more of their sides rather than of their tops. The map view, in effect, is a vertical view of all detail simultaneously.

The effects of image displacement can be held to a minimum in distance measure by using only a four- or five-inch square from the center of each print. This is normally possible with a full sequence of photos. It also helps just to be aware of the possibility of a rather large error.

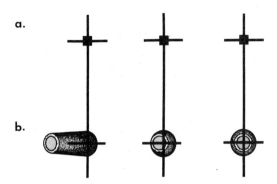

Figure 73. A comparison of map (*a*) and photo (*b*) of the same three structures. The photo view is centered directly over the smokestack in the lower right-hand corner. Note the scale distortion of the top of each stack as the images become more distant from photo center. The map view is centered over *each* placement.

Since photographs are not provided with handy bar scales as are most maps, distance measure becomes a bit more work with photo scale. Measured photo distance must be multiplied by the scale reciprocal, then converted into meaningful units. If, for example, the user finds a pair of photo images to be three inches apart on a photograph with a scale of 1:12000, he would compute ground distance between them in this way:

$$3'' \times 12,000 = 36,000''$$

and, converting inches to feet,

$$12\overline{)36,000''}^{3,000 \text{ ft.}}$$

or, a little over one half of a mile.

245

While useless for matters of point position, photo scale at least allows the navigator to think in round numbers. Without it, or without a great deal of experience in relating photos to the ground, it would be difficult to say that a particular pair of ground features were two or twenty miles apart.

Appendix

1. BEARINGS IN QUADRANT FORM

The quadrant system of naming compass directions divides the compass circle into four quarters, or "quadrants." Clockwise, these are NE, SE, SW, and NW.

Unlike the 360° azimuth scale, no quadrant bearing can be greater than 90°. Counting in any quadrant starts at the north-south line and proceeds either east or west up to 90° (*Figure 74* and *75*). The letters identifying the particular quadrant involved are always included in the written or spoken form; a bearing of 15° to the east of True North is written N 15° E and spoken "north fifteen degrees east." (This is equivalent to an azimuth of 15°.) A bearing of N 15° *W* is fifteen degrees to the *left* of the north-south line. (Equivalent to an azimuth of 345°.) Corresponding 15° bearings are also found in the two southern quadrants.

While the quadrant form is far less used than the azimuth, it does have several distinct advantages.

• Quadrant bearings are never over two digits, making them easier to manipulate.

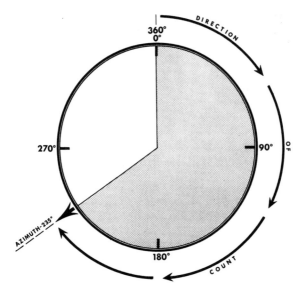

Figure 74. The azimuth numbering system, which utilizes the 360° of the circle as a unit, is the one used on most compasses. An azimuth is popularly, though erroneously, called a "bearing."

• Each bearing has three parts, each of which narrows down the part of the compass circle in which the bearing will be found; the first letter designates one half (N or S) of the circle; the last letter establishes the quadrant; and the number pinpoints the angle from True North or True South. The whole effect is to communicate orientation in stages. The whereabouts, for example, of an *azimuth* of 157° is a moment in coming through, but

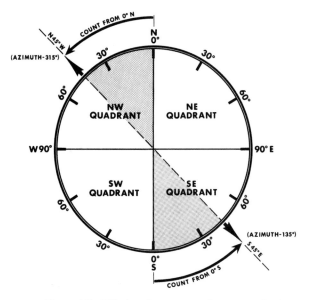

Figure 75. The bearing, or quadrant, numbering system. Bearings of up to 90° may be counted in any of the four quadrants. Each is uniquely identified by its two cardinal letters.

the same direction in quadrant form is rapidly communicated in a series of informative commands. It is S 23° E, an angle of 23° (toward the east) measured from True South on the compass card.

• The back bearing in quadrant form is the exact same degree value, but in the diagonally opposite quadrant. Thus, the back bearing of S 23° E is N 23° W.

Converting from quadrant form to azimuth form

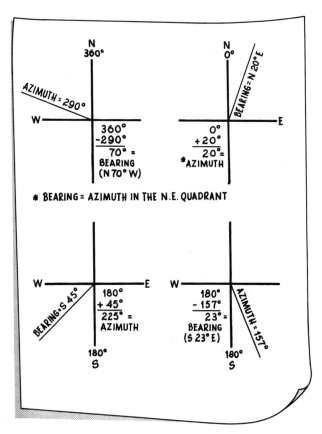

Figure 76. When making conversions from bearing to azimuth form or vice versa, simple sketches help to prevent quadrant errors and make it clear whether one must add or subtract degrees.

is a matter of arithmetic. It is always well to make a simple sketch first (*Figure 76*), for this will prevent many mistakes concerning the particular quadrant being used. In the case of S 23° E the sketch will show the bearing to lie on the right-hand side of the north-south line, which in azimuth form we know to be at 180°. Subtracting 23° from 180° yields an azimuth of 157°. Similar relationships exist around the compass circle; the back bearing of N 23° W lies 23° to the left of True North (which is either 360° or 0°, depending on which way one is counting). 360° minus 23° equals an azimuth of 337°.

Bearings in quadrant form are infrequently found in sport navigating on land (though more often in boating) but should be recognized and understood by all who fancy themselves familiar with the compass.

2. "SIMPLIFIED" COMPASS NAVIGATION

Confusion in reading and using the compass often centers around magnetic declination. The process for handling it differs according to whether one is taking or using a bearing and also whether one is in an area of east or west declination. No wonder few beginners really understand what is happening!

All Type A and most Type C compasses can be read directly in True terms; *for these the simplest method is explained in Chapters 2 and 4.* Any compass, however, can be used to navigate by magnetic bearings alone. The Type B model is particularly well suited for this approach since it can only be read in magnetic terms. If you care to try it with Types A or C, read either of these instruments while 0° is lined up with the compass needle. (Any model with a declination setscrew must of course be set to zero declination.)

Simplified compass navigation consists of using magnetic rather than True bearings, thereby avoiding the troublesome conversion process. For immediate use in the field — that is, when the navigator takes a bearing, walks the point-line, then takes another bearing and so on — it really makes little difference whether a direction is called X° True or Y° Magnetic. And for map work the map itself is easily converted to a magnetic orientation by adding a pencil line which amounts to a *magnetic meridian*. This is simply a line which crosses a True meridian at an angle equal to the magnetic declination for the particular sheet. Each time the map is to be oriented in the field the magnetic needle of the compass is aligned with the magnetic meridian before readings are taken from the compass card. The pencil line need not be drawn if the declination is kept in mind each time the map is oriented.

The drawback in the magnetic method is the changeable nature of magnetic declination (discussed in Chapter 5). Were this not the case, maps and recorded navigational information would indeed be written in magnetic terms.* For short periods of time, such as those involved with the usual outdoor route plan, the amount of change in declination is normally insignificant, but sooner or later the wilderness navigator will encounter a

---

* The aviator will quickly note that aeronautical charts do provide magnetic bearings, but he will also know that such charts are updated frequently and contain stern warnings not to use previous editions.

bearing which must be converted to or from one form or the other. The author takes the point of view that the 'simpler' method is the one which works in all cases.

3. TABLE OF MAGNETIC-TRUE CONVERSIONS

When the conversion is from:

MAG TO TRUE
(taking a bearing)

TRUE TO MAG
(using a bearing)

ADD east dec.	SUBTRACT west dec.	SUBTRACT east dec.	ADD west dec.

Do not memorize the entire table. If you live in an area of west declination the chances are that you will never have to deal with east declination and vice versa. That eliminates half of the table, leaving only two factors to learn—going from Mag to True and back to Mag. These two processes are exact opposites of one another, so really then, there is only *one* phrase to know by heart. For example, with east declination, drill it into yourself that "Mag to True" means to "add east" (when *taking* a bearing). It follows that in order to convert back to the magnetic form which the compass uses, you must "subtract east" (when *using* the bearing). Once the phrase "Mag to True—add east" is firmly in mind, the process for west declination is easily derived should it be required. "Add east" becomes "*subtract* west" in the same case of taking a bearing.

4. COMPASS COURSES: FUN AND INSTRUCTION

A course is a way or a route. Routes established for fun or instruction are apt to be quite different from those laid out for more serious route-finding. They are, in fact, much like a bicycle with training wheels; one does go through the motions, but he does not really learn how to ride until they have been taken off. More important, one does not learn how to fall. Training wheels do, however, build confidence.

The fact that compass courses are designed to teach gives them an inescapable air of the artificial. This stems from the amount of control which must be built into them. There is control over the kinds of reference features used, and control over the distances involved; there is usually an exaggerated control over the layout of the route segments in order to cover as many navigational problems as possible. Often, written directions are provided at turning points. All of these, along with supervision and coaching, restricted area, and parlor-games objectives, are the "training wheels" of a compass course.

The control which makes compass courses workable may also make them more difficult than many nonpractice situations. The navigator must often contend with boulders rather than bluffs, with shrubs rather than lonesome old pines, and with stakes in the ground rather than lofty peaks. Although in the wilds he will find no written directions—no hand-lettered bearing cards tacked to trees—neither will he ever have to search for "identifiable terrain features" in brush clumps and under juniper bushes as is sometimes the case with compass courses.

Compass courses are of two basic designs. The participant may be asked to *follow a planned route* and to locate unknown points, or he may be given a set of objectives and a map and asked to *plan the route* himself. Courses can be run against time (or another team) or for a point total, or they can be run simply to demonstrate the ability to do so. The first design, route following, is a technical test of ability to follow navigational directions. Route planning, on the other hand, is a test of the more advanced ability to make route-finding decisions. When navigational problems are realistic, either design tests leadership ability.

Not all compass courses need to be highly structured, nor are they all laid out for large groups. The *compass walk* is a simple individual exercise which can be made as complex as the navigator wishes, yet takes no equipment or preparation other than the compass itself. A compass walk is a traverse of a geometric figure, the simplest of which is an equal-sided triangle.

The bearings for traversing any *equal-angled* figure may be obtained by dividing 360° by the number of sides of the figure. The result is the amount which must be added to the previous bearing at each turn. For example, if a triangle traverse is begun on a bearing of 70°, the second leg will be on a bearing of 70° + 120°, and the third leg, back to the starting point, will be on a bearing of 190° + 120°. Each turn of the three-sided figure increases by one-third of the full 360°. To keep the arithmetic simple, begin with a bearing of 90° or

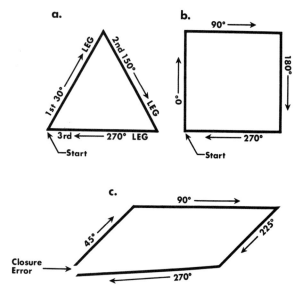

Figure 77. Compass walks or traverses are good
practice. Note the "error of closure" in *c*. This
error will occur more often than not, but the
smaller the error the better the job of navigating.

under. This avoids adding past the 360° mark.
One can add, say, 120° to 338° to obtain a last bearing (of 98°) but it is unnecessarily messy.

Figures such as the parallelogram in *Figure 77*
are more difficult to plot. In this case the bearings
for each pair of equal sides are reciprocals. An initial sketch is always a good investment in time.

Since the object of a compass walk is to "close"
back on the starting point (again, *see Figure 77*) the
difficulty of such an exercise will increase with the

number of sides, the lengths of the sides, and the complexity of the figure chosen. Figures of unequal side lengths are quite difficult, but in the final analysis afford the best practice. Part one of the trick is to walk the correct bearing, and part two is to measure the walking distance accurately. The beginning navigator should start with small and uncomplicated geometric figures, ones whose sides are short enough to allow direct sightings on each corner's objective. With mastery of these, distances should be lengthened until corners are out of sight from one another.

Distance measure is critical to the running of a compass course. Accuracy is usually either an objective in itself or is important in locating specified objectives. The method of pace counting, rejected as too monotonous for field work, is well suited for use in practice situations. Some of the drudgery of counting is lessened by using a double pace length as a measure; that is, right foot back to right foot as one pace.

Here is how to determine your double pace: First, lay out an accurately measured distance of 200 feet, then walk it several times, recording the number of double paces each time. Take the number which turns up most frequently and divide 200 by it. This will be your *pace-length factor,* or the distance in feet which you cover with one double pace.

For a sample computation let us suppose that you walked the 200 feet seven times and came out with these figures: 40, 36, 41, 40, 40, 39, and 40. Discount the 36 as a probable counting error. Of the remaining six figures, 40 turns up four times and is likely the most accurate count. Now, 200 feet divided by 40 paces = 5 feet per pace. To use this pace-length factor to lay out, say, a 350-foot line, you would have to first divide 350 by 5 to obtain the correct number of paces to step off. In the reverse procedure, to measure the length of a given line, you would first pace it off, then *multiply* the number of paces by the pace-length factor.

It is a good idea to record your own pace-length factor on or in some piece of equipment which is likely to be with you at any time in the wilderness. It can, for example, be scratched into your compass housing or written with indelible ink on your canteen cover.

Sloped ground will affect the length of your strides, but unless the particular stretch is all uphill or all downhill, pace-lengths will even out and slope can be ignored. If slope is all one way or the other, then some allowance for its effects must be made, especially if the distance is great. In compass courses the chances are good that the same error will have been made when the course was laid out.

One of the difficulties in running a compass course is in the detouring of obstacles without losing the bearing or fouling up the distance measure. *Figure 78* illustrates the most accurate method to use.

1. The navigator makes a turn of 90° from the point-line and counts paces until he has cleared the obstacle on the near side. (This count is *not* part of the distance measure along the bearing.)

2. He resumes the original bearing and pace-count parallel to the blocked point-line, walking until the obstacle is cleared in the forward direction.

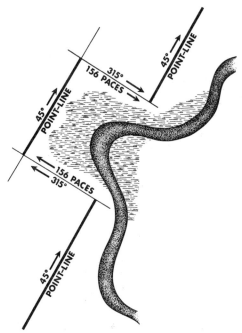

Figure 78. Detouring an obstacle has the effect of moving a section of the point-line to where the going is better.

3. He makes a 90° turn back toward the point-line, this time equaling the number of paces he stepped off away from it earlier. The pacing and counting along the original point-line are resumed.

The whole thing is much like the old Mutt and Jeff routine where Jeff has lost a quarter in the middle of the block but is looking for it under the street light on the corner because the light is better! If you cannot follow your point-line in one place, you simply move a piece of it to a location where the going is better.

Here are some general tips for running compass courses:

• Sight each bearing and back bearing a number of times to be sure. A degree or two will be important.

• Work with a partner if possible. One member of the team can remain at the last certain point until the partner either chooses an intermediary objective on the point-line (using the stationary teammate to line up on) or else locates the objective of that leg of the course.

• When distance has been measured as best as one can, and the objective is not yet found, *mark the spot,* then search closely and in a pattern. (Remember, the objective in a compass course may be a small stake or a flag.) One pattern of search is that of walking successively larger squares around the marked spot. Circles cannot be controlled for distance and bearing and the tendency is to become more and more confused. This squaring technique is also used to locate elusive supply caches, campsites, and lost articles—or anything which has no prominent landmark in association with it.

• Use the maximum possible straight-line distance before losing sight of the starting point.

5. COMPASS FEATURES TO LOOK FOR WHEN BUYING

There are dozens of sport compasses on the market today. They fit all needs and all pocketbooks. Within arbitrary limits of quality none is necessarily better than any other, and I will not attempt to recommend one particular make.

For most wilderness travel, and especially for the beginner, a liquid filled (damped) TYPE A compass with a standard clockwise (azimuth) numbering system will be a wise selection. The reasons for this choice will be given along with the list of recommended compass features.

If you already own a compass, *do not* buy a different one for any of the reasons given here. The most basic compass compares favorably with the most sophisticated in terms of results. Added features show their worth mainly in ease of operation, and it is doubtful if they ever make the difference between success and failure. Once familiar with your own compass it will be the one easiest for you to use.

It will also serve you well to buy an instrument first hand rather than by mail. It is not possible to put such qualities as readability, compactness, general feel, etc., into a catalog any more than it is possible to put them into the tabular form below. When a new model is considered, the following evaluation will serve as a guide. The features are noted in the order the author would weight their importance if he were selecting a compass.

Compass type. The TYPE A is preferred primarily because it yields True bearings with no extra effort. Most models are in the middle price range, from $5 to $9. The TYPE C compass (Forester or Cruiser), while usually in a higher price bracket, is also an excellent choice. It is more versatile than the TYPE

A, though for sporting use the added features are of doubtful value.

Damped needle. Liquid damping is given the edge over mechanical damping of the needle's oscillations. The friction offered by the liquid is on the job at all times, while a mechanical damper gives the operator one more thing to do during the sighting. Mechanical damping's one advantage may be that it can be used to manually hold the needle in place for a closer look at the reading once the instrument has been steadied. On the other hand, compasses with direction-of-travel arrows allow the same close reading with no holding of the needle necessary.

Direction-of-travel arrow. The DOT arrow is a decided advantage, particularly in that it marks the place on the dial one is considering. If the eye or the needle is allowed to wander, the arrow is still in place for a quick return to business.

Tick spacing. A space of 2° between shown tick-marks is favored. 1° ticks are too close for the eye to separate quickly, while 5° or 10° spacing leaves too much guess work, especially where accuracy is critical (such as in compass courses.) The eye easily halves a 2° space with more than equal the accuracy of any sighting with a hand-held compass.

Declination Setscrew. Helpful but not really necessary, at least with TYPE A compasses. Saves confusion in reading TYPE C models, most of which have devices to offset declination.

Scale: azimuth or bearing? The azimuth scale is far more widely used. The bearing scale is a useful extra feature, and all who use a compass should know how it works. Some compasses have only the cardinal or intercardinal points on the dial with few tickmarks in between. If your wilderness pursuit requires anything more than finding general directions, these should be avoided.

Protractor base. The protractor base also falls into the "useful" category. It is of most help in map work, especially when made of a transparent material. Such bases usually are imprinted with a DOT arrow; however, the watchcase styles of TYPE A may contain DOT arrows and are far less bulky to store and carry.

Price. Price must, of course, be judged according to means. Some models selling for as little as $3 have as many features from this list as do compasses of four times the price. They will, however, lack some in durability and in quality of materials and workmanship. Price alone is a poor yardstick, but like a corral fence, it at least shows where to start looking for the one you want. Those instruments in the middle price range should be most seriously considered.

Style. Compasses come in many styles—pocket, wrist, pin-on, etc.—and the selection of one over the other may be a matter of preference. One of the conventional pocket models, which can be stowed away when not in use, is suggested. Wrist models become buried under tight cuffs, and pin-ons are easily torn off by brush.

Sighting arrangement. Sights are helpful but not essential by any means. The only effective sighting arrangement the author is familiar with is that used on the lensatic (TYPE B) compass; however, that feature is decidedly not enough to suggest its purchase over a wide range of TYPES A and C.

Luminous dial. One is forced to consider that luminous dials may add something to a commando raid, but little to recreational woodsmanship. Most are nearly impossible to read by their own light, especially after a few years old. The military lensatic model has a special luminous course-setter which can be preset in the light to be read in the dark when a critical turning point is reached. We woods-bunny types, however, should hole up long before navigation becomes that serious.

6. SUGGESTED READING

Each of the books on the following list was chosen because it deepens one's understanding of one or more topics discussed in this one. Any or all of them make excellent additions to a permanent outdoor activities library.

Gardner, Allan C.
A Short Course in Navigation
Funk & Wagnalls, N.Y. 1968

Garland, Lt. Albert N., editor and publisher
Leader's Handbook, 4th edition, July 1967
Available for $.50 plus $.10 handling from:
   Infantry Magazine Book Store,
   U.S. Army Infantry School,
   Ft. Benning, Georgia 31905

Gatty, Harold
Nature Is Your Guide
E. P. Dutton Co. N.Y. 1958

Kjellstrom, Bjorn
Be Expert With Map and Compass
American Orienteering Service, Laporte, Indiana
revised 1967

Lehr, Paul E., R. Will Burnett, and Herbert S. Zim
Weather, a Guide to Phenomena and Forecasts, a Golden
Science Guide, Golden Press, New York, 1965.

Manning, Harvey, Chairman of the editors
Mountaineering, the Freedom of the Hills
The Mountaineers, Seattle, Washington, 1969

Miracle, Leonard, with Maurice Decker
Complete Book of Camping
Outdoor Life-Harper & Row, N.Y., 1961

Ratliff, Donald E.
Map, Compass, and Campfire
Binfords & Mort, Portland, Oregon, 1964

Rutstrum, Calvin
The Wilderness Route Finder
Macmillan Co., N.Y., 1967

Index